First Year Student Library Instruction Programs
CLIP Note #33

Compiled by

Debbie Malone
DeSales University
Center Valley, Pennsylvania

Carol Videon
Delaware County Community College
Media, Pennsylvania

College Library Information Packet Committee
College Libraries Section
Association of College and Research Libraries
A Division of the American Library Association
Chicago 2003

The paper used in this publication meets the minimum requirements of American National Standard for Information Sciences–Permanence of Paper for Printed Library Materials, ANSI Z39.48-1992. ∞

Library of Congress Cataloging-in-Publication Data
Library of Congress Cataloging-in-Publication Data

First year student library instruction programs / compiled by Debbie Malone, Carol Videon.
    p. cm. -- (CLIP note ; #33)
Includes bibliographical references.
 ISBN 0-8389-8230-1 (alk. paper)
 1. Library orientation for college students--United States. 2. Information literacy--Study and teaching (Higher)--United States. I. Malone, Debbie. II. Videon, Carol. III. Series: CLIP notes ; #33.

Z711.2.F56 2003
027.6'2'0973--dc21

               2003011039

Printed on recycled paper.

Printed in the United States of America.

07 06 05 04   5 4 3 2

TABLE OF CONTENTS

        Goshen College
        Harold and Wilma Good Library
        Goshen, Indiana

        Lafayette College
        Skillman Library
        Easton, Pennsylvania

        Lynchburg College
        Knight-Capron Library
        Lynchburg, Virginia

Messiah College
Murray Library
Grantham, Pennsylvania

North Central College
North Central College Library
Naperville, Illinois

Reed College
Reed College Library
Portland, Oregon

Seton Hill University
Reeves Library
Greensburg, Pennsylvania

Shawnee State University
Clark Memorial Library
Portsmouth, Ohio

University of Richmond
Boatwright Memorial Library
Richmond, Virginia

Wartburg College
Vogel Library
Waverly, Iowa

Wheaton College
Bushwell Memorial Library
Wheaton, Illinois

Western New England College
D'Amour Library
Springfield, Massachusetts

William Patterson College
David and Lorraine Cheng Library
Wayne, New Jersey

Arkansas Tech University
Pendergraft Library and Technology Center
Russellville, Arkansas

Birmingham Southern College
Miles Library
Birmingham, Alabama

California State University San Marcos
Cal State San Marcos Library
San Marcos, California

Gannon University
Nash Library
Erie, Pennsylvania

Lynchburg College
Knight-Capron Library
Lynchburg, Virginia

St. Francis University
Pasquerilla Library
Loretto, Pennsylvania

Wayne State University
Walter P. Reuther Library
Detroit, Michigan

University of North Carolina Asheville
D. Hiden Ramsey Library
Asheville, North Carolina

University of North Florida
Thomas G. Carpenter Library
Jacksonville, Florida

York College
Schmidt Library
York, Pennsylvania

Goucher College
Julia Rogers Library
Baltimore, Maryland

North Central College
North Central College Library
Naperville, Illinois

Northern State University
Williams Library
Aberdeen, South Dakota

University of Montevallo
Carmichael Library
Montevallo, Alabama

University of Richmond
Boatwright Memorial Library
Richmond, Virginia

University of Southern Colorado
University Library
Pueblo, Colorado

Xavier University
University Library
Cincinnati, Ohio

Austin College
Abell Library
Sherman, Texas

Earlham College
Lilly Library
Richmond, Indiana

Eckerd College
Eckerd College Library
St. Petersburg, Florida

Goshen College
Harold and Wilma Good Library
Goshen, Indiana

Lynchburg College
Knight-Capron Library
Lynchburg, Virginia

Marywood University
Marywood University Library
Scranton, Pennsylvania

Salisbury University
Blackwell Library
Salisbury, Maryland

SUNY College Fredonia
State University of New York
Daniel A. Reed Library
Fredonia, New York

University of North Carolina Pembroke
Sampson-Livermore Library
Pembroke, North Carolina

Walla Walla College
Peterson Memorial Library
College Place, Washington

CLIP NOTES COMMITTEE

David A. Wright, Chair
Speed Library
Mississippi College
Clinton, Mississippi

Rhonna A. Goodman
Manhattanville College Library
Manhattanville College
Purchase, New York

David P. Jensen
Van Wylen Library
Hope College
Holland, Michigan

Jean Lacovara
Mariam Coffin Canaday Library
Bryn Mawr College
Bryn Mawr, Pennsylvannia

Christopher B. Loring
Smith College Libraries
Smith College
Northampton, Massachusetts

Nancy Newins
McGraw-Page Library
Randolph-Macon College
Ashland, Virginia

Jennifer Phillips
University Library Services
Virginia Commonwealth University
Richmond, Virginia

Brian Rossmann
Montana State University Libraries
Montana State University
Billings, Montana

Gene Ruffin
Gwinnett University Library
Gwinnett University
Lawrenceville, Georgia

Marcia L. Thomas
Ames Library
Illinois Wesleyan University
Bloomington, Illinois

Ann Watson
Denison University Libraries
Denison University
Granville, Ohio

Corey Williams-Green
Russell D. Cole Library
Cornell College
Mount Vernon, Iowa

Thanks to Phyllis Vogel, DeSales Technical Services Librarian, who provided invaluable help in mailing the surveys and proofreading the documents, and to Len Davidson, DeSales Systems Librarian, who was patient and tireless in working through document and word processing problems. Special thanks to Dan Zarenkiewicz and Jason Barnes, DeSales workstudy students, who entered our data so accurately.

INTRODUCTION

OBJECTIVE

The College Library Information Packet (CLIP) Notes publishing program, under the auspices of the College Libraries Section of the Association of College and Research Libraries, provides "college and small university libraries with state-of-the-art reviews and current documentation on library practices and procedures of relevance to them." (Morein 226). This CLIP NOTE provides information on first year student library instruction.

BACKGROUND

Since the 1970's college librarians have been working with faculty to incorporate library instruction into their courses. (Kelly 77) The professional literature provides examples of librarians teaming with faculty to integrate library instruction into freshmen composition courses (Gauss 17) as well as librarians who have successfully built library instruction into first year seminar or symposium courses which are part of the college's core requirements for all students (Blakeslee 73, Nugent 147, Parang 270, Parks 65, Sonntag and Weinberg 4). The literature also includes discussions of separate stand-alone credit courses that have been created by librarians for entry-level students. (Alexander 245 and Poirer 233).

The focus here is on first year students because so many instruction sessions are integrated into first year student courses, particularly English and writing courses, and this provides an opportunity to provide basic skills to a broad range of students at the beginning of their academic careers.

Since the publication of ACRL's Objectives for Information Literacy Instruction: a Model Statement for Academic Librarians (ACRL) in 2001 librarians have an updated tool to assist them in planning many forms of instruction. It is not yet entirely clear how extensively these objectives have been integrated at colleges and universities across the country. This study provides examples of goals and objectives from a variety of institutions in a wide variety of instructional settings. In some of these institutions, information literacy skills are sequenced through several courses over the course of the student's college experience.

Online tutorials show great promise for instruction in terms of covering basic skills, providing opportunities for active student participation and self-paced study. Documents included here provide examples of varied approaches taken by our respondents.

Stand-alone information literacy courses for First Year Students are not widely offered by our survey respondents, but the syllabi included here display the depth of instruction possible through elective or required courses.

Library instruction classroom exercises or worksheets can provide active learning opportunities for students and numerous examples are provided here.

SURVEY PROCEDURE

The authors used the standard procedure for CLIP Note surveys. After the initial proposal and draft of the survey were submitted to ACRL'S Clip Note Committee for approval, surveys were mailed to participants in August of 2002. A second mailing was sent out in October, 2002 and a third mailing in November, 2002. Responses were accepted through December, 2002.

ANALYSIS OF SURVEY RESULTS

General Information on the Survey

Surveys were sent to 292 colleges and universities, 153 of which responded, representing a response rate of 53%. The institutions ranged in size from student bodies of 585 FTE to 17, 262 FTE. For purposes of analysis of some survey responses by size of institution, the institutions were grouped into the following categories:

1000 or fewer	11% (N=17)
1001-3000	55% (N=84)
3001-5000	20% (N=30)
over 5000	14% (N=22)

Instruction Librarians and Sessions Taught

Number of FTE Librarians (Questions 3-4)

The average number of FTE librarians in respondents' institutions was 7.5 librarians. The low end of the range was 2 and the high was 24.72. This does not represent a normal distribution; a few schools with many librarians brought the mean higher. This average does correlate with the 7.68 average number of librarians which Merz and Mark found in their CLIP Note survey done in 2001. [1]

The average number of librarians participating in instruction as some part of their jobs was 4.75 which represents 63% of all librarians in these institutions. This compares with Merz and Mark's finding that and average of 5.33 (or 69%) of librarians are involved in instruction.[2]

The size of the institutions clearly had an effect on the ratio of instructional librarians to students. In larger schools with over 5000 students the ratio was 1278:1; in schools with 3001-5000 students the ration was 902:1; in schools with 1001-3000 students the ratio was 610:1; and in smaller schools with 1000 or fewer students the ration was 384:1. Larger schools in general may have larger classes and this extends to library instruction as well. The overall ratio of students to teaching librarians was 745:1.

How many course-related sessions are offered for First Year Students? (Question 5)

The number of course-related sessions (separate from stand alone credit courses) taught by respondents varied greatly by size of institutions, as would be expected. Schools with 1000 or fewer students taught an average of 30.5 sessions per year; schools with 1001-3000 students taught 39.3 sessions per year; schools with 3001-5000 students taught 53.4 sessions; and larger schools taught an average of 102.9 sessions.

---

[1] Merz and Mark <u>Assessment in College Library Instruction Programs</u> pg. 3
[2] Ibid. pg. 3

In general, librarians at smaller institutions are teaching slightly more sessions *per student* than their colleagues at larger schools. Librarians at institutions of 1000 or few students taught 1.9 sessions per First Year Student; schools with 1001-3000 taught 1.7 sessions; schools with 3001-5000 taught 1.3 sessions; and larger schools taught 1.4 sessions per First Year Student.

How many institutions are offering credit bearing stand-alone courses for First Year Students? (Question 6)

Our survey results indicated that relatively few institutions offer separate credit bearing library instruction courses for First Year Students. Six institutions provide a required credit stand-alone course and ten institutions provide an elective stand-alone course. In two of these institutions the course is required for some majors and not required for others. A number of institutions said that they provide credit courses which are open to upper level students as well as first year students, and we did not include them in these totals.

Two institutions provide interesting variations. One school provides six sessions which are integrated into five different general education courses and includes a separate grade for the library portion. The greatest reported weakness with this program is that "It is dependent on each faculty [member] to incorporate in the best way possible. New faculty are reluctant at first. The strength is that it is 100% integrated into the curriculum." The second institution provides both an elective credit course and a sequence of four sessions in two required English courses.

One librarian whose institution has been providing a required credit information literacy course for five years stated that the strengths of the program are that students develop basic competencies to locate, evaluate and use information in many situations, but the biggest weakness is that First Year Students do not always appreciate the need for these skills until later in their careers.

Another respondent said that although they now provide a stand-alone credit course for First Year Students, they are working to integrate the course as an information literacy unit within the broader context of a required language course. That is an interesting concept which could be researched further.

How is instruction delivered to First Year Students? (Question 7)

The most frequently reported type of instruction provided was the one-class course related library session, with 129 institutions, or 84.3% of our respondents, indicating they provide this type of instruction. Relatively few institutions are providing web based virtual library tours or audio tours.

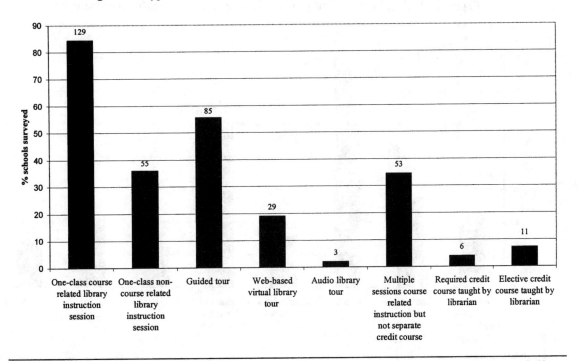

Figure A. Types of formal library instruction provided to first year students

---

How many institutions have written and articulated statements of competencies or skill objectives for First Year Students? (Question 8)

Only about one third of our respondents (51 of 153 institutions) indicated that they had written statements of competency or skill goals for First Year Students. The size of the institution did not seem to play a role.

Are library skills an articulated objective or competency in any required general curriculum courses for First Year Students? (Question 9)

In 46.4% of responding institutions, library skills are clearly articulated for at least some courses required of First Year Students. However, 53.6% schools surveyed said that either they did not know of such defined competencies or their institutions did not delineate information literacy goals for first year courses.

What types of assignments/projects are assigned as part of library instruction for First Year Students? (Question 10)

The most frequently noted type of assignment was the bibliography (108 institutions or 70.6%) followed closely by the annotated list of sources (71 institutions or 46.4 %). Thirty-two institutions said they were using online tutorials as a regular part of their First Year Student instruction.

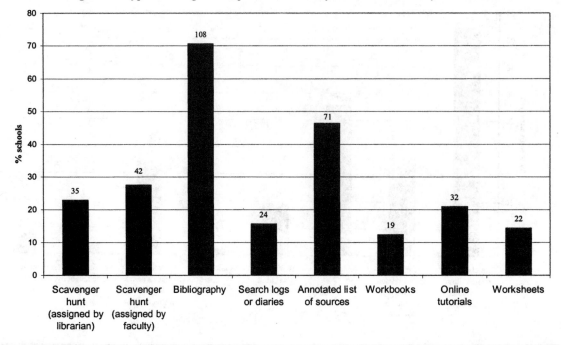

Figure B. Types of assignments provided in first year students' library instruction

Twenty-two respondents indicated that they created detailed exercises for students to begin during the "hands-on" portion of the instruction session, and many of them provided us with useful examples. This trend seemed significant and so another response was added to the survey tally to record this data.

Who is responsible for grading/evaluating student work done as part of a library assignment? (Question 11)

The most frequent response was that faculty members do most of the grading (seventy-nine), and fifty-four respondents said that grading is not done for their library sessions. Fifty-three institutions reported that librarians do the grading. Four institutions mentioned that their students take online quizzes which are graded by the computer.

What types of multi-media technology are used in instruction for First Year Students? (Question 12)

Our respondents are frequently using technology to enhance their instruction. A projected demonstration of a database (133 or 86.8%) and hands-on practice at a computer (132 or 86.3%) were the two most often used technologies. Fifty-eight institutions create web pages for particular classes, and eighty-three respondents (54.3%) incorporate PowerPoint presentations in their instruction.

Figure C. Types of multi-media technology used in instruction for first year students

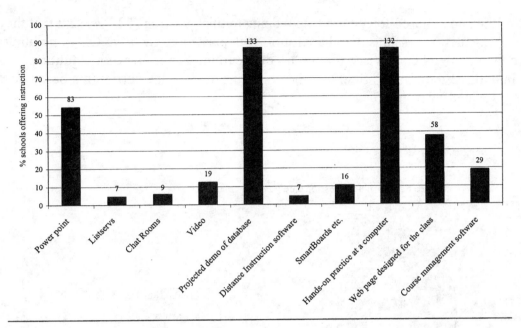

What is the class size that occurs most frequently in instruction sessions for First Year Students? (Question 13)

In an encouraging trend 72.4% (110 respondents) reported that their class size was generally between 16 and 25 students. Only 20 institutions (13.2%) indicated that their classes were generally over 25 students.

Figure D. Most frequently occuring class size

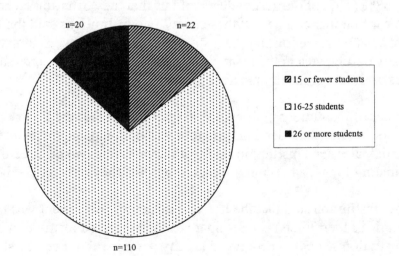

Who is generally responsible for planning instruction sessions for First Year Students?
(Question 14)

A majority of the one hundred forty-nine respondents to this question (59.7%) said that they generally plan instruction sessions in collaboration with classroom faculty. Only one library said that the faculty members devised the library curriculum. A number of institutions mentioned in notes in the "Other" field that the librarians devised the curriculum based on assignments provided by instructors.

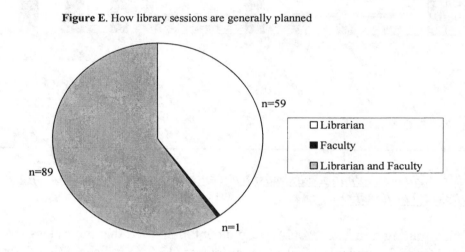

Figure E. How library sessions are generally planned

n=59

n=89

n=1

□ Librarian
■ Faculty
▨ Librarian and Faculty

How many institutions offer instruction as part of a First Year Seminar and how are they generally taught? (Questions 15 and 18)

About 68% (105) of our respondents told us that they offer library instruction as part of a First Year Seminar course. Of these, sixty-two institutions said the faculty member is usually present as an observer during the instruction, and thirty-two said that the faculty member generally participates in the instruction. Only eleven respondents said that the librarian teaches without the faculty member present.

A number of institutions commented in question 18 that the library component of their institution's First Year Seminar program was optional and that some instructors therefore did not participate. One institution said that they provide two or three library sessions for each participating First Year Seminar section, but that they only reached one-third of all sections.

Another institution said that the library instruction component was not required but about two-thirds of their First Year Seminar sections received instruction because the administration strongly encouraged faculty participation. Each First Year Seminar that was involved in information literacy had a librarian assigned to it who worked with the faculty member on assignments, presentations, etc. to incorporate information literacy into the course. A second respondent provided three online learning modules with quizzes graded as part of a First Year Seminar, and reinforcing library assignments were created by each participating faculty member. One weakness in this process was that with so many different instructors and topics, there were various levels of success in the ways the assignments reinforced the use of the particular library resources introduced in the online tutorials.

A third institution mentioned that variability in learning goals across their First Year Seminar sections was a weakness. A related problem discussed by other librarians was that some First Year Seminar sections at their institutions were very research intensive and others much less so, which made library instruction more difficult. A number of respondents said that although library instruction was a required part of the First Year Seminar, some instructors still failed to participate.

How many institutions offer multiple course-related sessions for First Year Students and how are these taught? (Question 16)

Only seventy-one (46.4 %) of our respondents indicated that they provide multiple course-related instruction sessions for First Year Students. Of these, 49.3% teach with the instructor participating and only 8.5% (6 responses) teach without the faculty member present in the classroom.

Figure F. How instruction sessions are generally taught in schools with multiple course-related instruction sessions

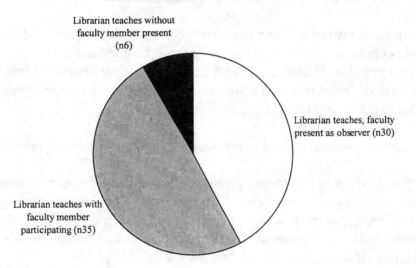

What do librarians see as the strengths and weaknesses of their overall program for First Year Students? (Question 18)

Program strengths fell into two major themes:

1. The major strength noted by numerous institutions was that their programs reached most, if not all, First Year Students. Even if students only had one library instruction session, some librarians reported satisfaction that the sessions helped overcome student hesitation about coming to the library and encouraged students to seek out librarians for assistance. One library reported success with an online tutorial and follow-up tour format. Another school felt that an online tutorial plus one or two course-related instruction sessions gave students a basic grounding.

2. Another encouraging strength some institutions mentioned was strong collaborative relationships with faculty and administration on their campuses. One institution stated that their General Education Committee had approved and adopted their information literacy objectives, and that after library instruction sessions, students must pass a twenty-five question test. They say, "We love this because students must pay attention!"

   One institution mentioned that both faculty and students warmly welcomed librarians into the classroom and that the institution had a consistently high participation rate with First Year Student program faculty. Another respondent said that librarians had a good relationship with faculty who use their services and that the number of course-related sessions they taught was rising. This seems to be a case of good library instruction followed by word-of-mouth publicity via the faculty.

   Some institutions stated that because of good faculty collaboration their three course-related sessions in a First Year course provided a good basis for instruction, review and hands-on practice. Another school noted that multiple course-related sessions provided time to use different teaching styles to address various learning styles and still provide time for practice and repetition.

Program weaknesses discussed by respondents fall into five major themes:

1. The most frequently mentioned problem was the lack of a requirement for library instruction in any course for First Year Students. The variable "buy-in" by faculty members results in inconsistent instruction for students. One institution said that some students receive instruction in three or four classes and other students never receive instruction - it depends on the classes they take.

   Other institutions said that information literacy was a requirement of some majors but not others, and a number of schools said that they miss transfer students who do not take some of the general education courses. One institution mentioned that some faculty provide their own research component for their students but that they are often not alert to changes in library resources.

One respondent summarized the problem succinctly: "We wish we could find a good way to reach all First Year Students. We've tried all kinds of things, but the perfect solution has eluded us."

2. Many institutions discussed a disconnect between library instruction and class assignments. One school mentioned that they incorporated an artificial assignment in their library instruction rather than an assignment integral to the course which they feel would better demonstrate the relevance of library skills to the curriculum. Similarly, another institution stated that although most faculty members stress the importance of library skills, they often have nothing to tie the library sessions to class work. Students therefore see the library as peripheral or "just another Liberal Arts Seminar thing we have to do."

3. Numerous institutions talked about the lack of sequenced, more in-depth instruction beyond the basic instruction provided for First Year Students. Some librarians saw "very little follow-up of students using these skills beyond the library sessions themselves." Other institutions had no strongly recommended or required next level of information literacy. This is clearly an area where strong leadership from library administrators needs to be encouraged. Librarians need to work with both faculty and their academic administrators to more fully integrate information literacy initiatives into the curriculum.

4. Too little class time with students was another commonly mentioned weakness in First Year Student instruction programs. Many institutions said that instruction was more superficial than they would like it to be. Schools providing only one-shot sessions with students stated that they could not integrate such things as critical thinking skills, more in-depth searching techniques, or more active learning exercises. One-shot sessions often prohibited the use of multiple teaching modalities and precluded the pedagogy of review and reinforcement. Even with two fifty minute sessions, many librarians said that they could not attain the breadth or depth of instruction that is necessary.

5. Fewer institutions mentioned staffing and facilities as major problems for their programs. However, those who did discuss staffing problems said that they could provide only basic instruction in single sessions or orientation tours and that they had little time or money to develop new presentations. One institution said that its instruction staff was inadequate due to growing enrollments.

    Some libraries that are short staffed said they have migrated to online teaching modules as a way to reach more students.

    Seven librarians said that they were hampered by inadequate access to computer labs for hands-on practice during their sessions, and another institution felt that the library needed to own or control its own computer lab.

Conclusion

With the changing environment of information literacy and the diversity among colleges and universities, there is no "one size fits all" model program. Variables to success depend on individual courses, individual instructors, the structure of the various disciplines, the administrative support and the climate of the university. Documents which provide samples of objectives, syllabi, assignments, and tutorials included here are offered as suggestions for librarians and faculty to test as they work together to provide effective instruction to reach a shared goal of graduating information literate students.

WORKS CITED

Alexander, Linda. "LME 101: A Required Course in Basic Library Skills." *Research Strategies* 13 (1995): 245-249.

ACRL. Objectives for Information Literacy Instruction: A Model Statement for Academic Librarians. Chicago: Association of College and Research Libraries, 2001. 28. Feb. 2003. <http://www.ala.org/acrl/guides/objinfolit.html>

Blakeslee, Sarah. "Librarian in a Strange Land: Teaching a Freshman Orientation Course." *Reference Services Review* 26 (1998), no. 2: 73-78.

Gauss, Nancy and William King. "Integrating Information Literacy Into Freshmen Composition: Beginning a Long and Beautiful Friendship." *Colorado Libraries* 24 no. 4 (1998): 17-20.

Kelly, Maurie Caitlin and Andrea Kross, eds. *Making the Grade: Academic Libraries and Student Success.* Chicago: Association of College and Research Libraries, 2002.

Merz, Lawrie H and Beth L. Mark. *Assessment in College Library Instruction Programs.* Chicago: Association of College and Research Libraries, 2002.

Morein, P. Grady. "What is a CLIP Note?" *College and Research Libraries News* 46 (1985): 226.

Nugent, Chris and Roger Myers. "Learning by Doing: the Freshmen-Year Curriculum and Library Instruction." *Research Strategies* 17 (2000): 147-155.

Parks, Joan and Dana Hendrix. "Integrating Library Instruction Into the Curriculum Through Freshman Symposium." *Reference Services Review 24 (*Spring 1996*)*: 65-72.

Poirier, Gayle. "Teaching Critical Thinking in a Library Credit Course." *Research Strategies* 11, no 4 (1993): 233-241.

Sonntag, Gabriela. "Using Technology in a First Year Experience Course." *College & Undergraduate Libraries* 6, no 1 (1999): 1-16.

Weinberg, Linda. *Report of the Committee to Develop the Library and Information Technology Session for the Freshman Experience.* Adelphi University, NY, (1999): ERIC Document Reproduction Service, ED437959.

TEXTBOOKS USED IN INFORMATION LITERACY COURSES

Badke, William. *Research Strategies: Finding Your Way Through the Information Fog.* Lincoln, NE: Writers Club Press, 2000. [last modified 8 Mar. 2002] 10 Mar. 2003 <www.acts.twu.ca/LBR/preface.htm>.

Blazek, Ron. *The Humanities: A Selective Guide to Information Sources.* Englewood: Libraries Unlimited, 2000.

Bolner, Myrtle S. and Gayle A. Poirer. *The Research Process: Books and Beyond.* Dubuque: Kendall/Hunt, 2002.

Campbell, Susan and Kimberley Donnelly and Steve Kirby. *IFL 101 eText.* York College, 2001. 10 Mar. 2003. < www.ycp.edu/library/ifl/etext/ethome.html>.

Comer, Douglas. *The Internet Book: Everything You Need To Know About Computer Networking and How the Internet Works.* Upper Saddle River: Prentice Hall, 2000.

Gates, Jean Key. *Guide to the Use of Libraries and Information Sources.* New York: McGraw-Hill, 1994.

Lawley, Elizabeth Lane. *Internet Primer for Information Professionals: a Basic Guide to Internet Networking Technology.* Westport: Meckler, 1993.

List, Carla. *Information Research.* Dubuque: Kendell/Hunt, 2002.

Mann, Thomas. *A Guide to Library Research Methods.* New York: Oxford University Press, 1987.

Mann, Thomas. *The Oxford Guide to Library Research.* New York: Oxford University Press, 1998.

Quaratiello, Arlene Rodda. *The College Student's Research Companion.* New York: Neal Schuman Publishers, 2000.

Radford, Marie L. and Susan B. Barnes and Linda R. Barr. *Web Research: Selecting, Evaluating, and Citing.* Boston: Allyn and Bacon, 2002.

Sinclair, Bryan, ed. *Making Sense of Library Research: A Guide for Undergraduate Students.* University of North Carolina at Asheville, 2001. 10 Mar. 2003 <bullpup.lib.unca.edu/library/lr/txtbk/txtbk.html>.

Watts, Margit Misangyi.. *College: We Make the Road by Walking.* Upper Saddle River, NJ: Prentice Hall, 2003.

SELECTED BIBLIOGRAPHY

SELECTED BIBLIOGRAPHY

ACRL Objectives for Information Literacy Instruction: A Model Statement for Academic Librarians. Chicago: Association of College and Research Libraries, 2001. 28. Feb. 2003. <http://www.ala.org/acrl/guides/objinfolit.html>

Alexander, Linda. "LME 101: A Required Course in Basic Library Skills." *Research Strategies* 13 (1995): 245-249.

Blakeslee, Sarah. "Librarian in a Strange Land: Teaching a Freshman Orientation Course." *Reference Services Review* 26, no. 2 (1998): 73-78.

Brown, Stephanie Willen and Bonnie Vigeland. "An Innovative First-Year Instruction Program at Hampshire College." *College & Research Libraries News* 62, no.7 (2001): 717-719.

Burtle, Laura G. and Tammy S. Sugarman. "The Citizen in the Information Age: Georgia State University's Creation of a Librarian-led Freshmen Learning Community." *College & Research Libraries News* 63, no.4 (2002): 276-279.

Coleman, Paul. "Give 'Em the Big Picture: Bibliographic Instruction for Freshmen Orientation". *Research Strategies* 4 (1986): 132-135.

Dabbour, Katherine Strob. "Applying Active Learning Methods to the Design of Library Instruction for a Freshman Seminar." *College and Research Libraries* 58, no. 4 (1997): 299-307.

Gauss, Nancy and William King. "Integrating Information Literacy into Freshmen Composition: Beginning a Long and Beautiful Friendship." *Colorado Libraries* 24, no. 4 (1998): 17-20.

Germain, Carol Anne, and Trudi E. Jackson and Sue A. Kaczor. "A Comparison of the Effectiveness of Presentation Formats for Instruction: Teaching First-Year Students." *College & Research Libraries* 61, no.1 (2000): 65.

Grassian , Esther G. and Joan R. Kaplowitz. *Information Literacy Instruction: Theory and Practice*. New York: Neal-Schuman Publishers, 2001.

Higgins, Carla and Mary Jane Cedar Face. "Integrating Information Literacy Skills into the University Colloquium: Innovation at Southern Oregon University." *Reference Services Review* 26, no. 3-4 (1998): 17-32.

Hull, Tracy L. and Kelley A. Lawton. "The Development of a First-Year Student Library Instruction Program at Duke University." *The Reference Librarian* 73 (2001): 323-336.

Jacobson, Trudi E. and Beth L. Mark. "Separating Wheat from Chaff: Helping First-Year Students Become Information Savvy." *The Journal of General Education* 49, no.4 (2000): 257-278.

Kelly, Maurie Caitlin and Andrea Kross, eds. *Making the Grade: Academic Libraries and Student Success*. Chicago: Association of College and Research Libraries, 2002.

Keyser, Marcia W. and Laura R. Lucio. "Adding a Library Instruction Unit to an Established Course." *Research Strategies* 16, no.3 (1998): 221-229.

Leckie, Gloria J. "Desperately Seeking Citations: Uncovering Faculty Assumptions about the Undergraduate Research Process." *The Journal of Academic Librarianship* 22, no.3 (1996): 201-208.

Merz, Lawrie H. and Beth L. Mark. 2002. *Assessment in College Library Instruction Programs*. Chicago: Association of College and Research Libraries, 2002.

Morein, P. Grady. "What is a CLIP Note?" *College and Research Libraries News* 46 (1985): 226.

Nims, Julia K. and Ann Andrew, eds. *First Impressions, Lasting Impact: Introducing the First-Year Student to the Academic Library*. Ann Arbor: Pierian Press, 2002.

Nugent, Chris and Roger Myers. "Learning By Doing: the Freshmen Year Curriculum and Library Instruction." *Research Strategies* 17 (2000): 147-155.

Parang, Elizabeth and Melinda Raine and Trisha Stevenson. "Redesigning Freshmen Seminar Library Instruction Based on Information Competencies." *Research Strategies* 17, no. 4 (2000): 269-280.

Parks, Joan and Dana Hendrix. "Integrating Library Instruction Into the Curriculum Through Freshmen Symposium." *Reference Services Review* 24 (Spring 1996): 65-72.

Poirier, Gayle. "Teaching Critical Thinking in a Library Credit Course." *Research Strategies* 11, no. 4 (1993): 233-241.

Sonntag, Gabriela. "Using technology in a First Year Experience Course." *College & Undergraduate Libraries* 6 (1999), no 1: 1-16.

St. Clair, Linda. "The 'LEAPing' Librarians Role in a Campus Learning Community: Helping Students Get Through their Freshman Year." *College & Research Library News* 63, no. 1 (2002): 24-26.

Sugarman, Tammy and Anne Page Mosby. "Making a Weak Link Stronger: Incorporating Information Literacy into a Semester-Long Freshman Seminar." *Georgia Library Quarterly* 39, no. 2 (2002): 12-16.

Wassermann, Carol E. "Life Skills 2000: an Introductory Workshop for Incoming Freshmen." *College and Undergraduate Libraries* 7, no.2 (2000): 11-22.

Weinberg, Linda, et al. *Report of the Committee to Develop the Library and Information Technology Session for the Freshmen Experience.* Adelphi University, NY: ERIC Document Reproduction Service, 1999. ED437959.

SURVEY DATA

First Year Library Instruction in College Libraries
CLIP NOTE Survey

Name of Person completing this survey_____

Title of Person completing this survey_____

General Data

1. Name of Institution_____
2. *Number of FTE students **median=2300; range=585-17,262** (153 responses)
3. *Number of FTE librarians **median=6; range=2-24.72** (153 responses)
4. The number of librarians participating in classroom instruction
        Median=4; range=1-17 (153 responses)
5. Total number of non-credit library instruction sessions taught for first year students per calendar year **median=37; range=0-235** (131 responses)
6. Total number of for-credit library instruction sessions taught for first year students per calendar year: (*respondents were confused with this question. We report below the number of institutions that indicated offering each type of stand alone credit course*)
    a. One credit course sessions **13**
    b. Two credit course sessions **2**
    c. Three credit course sessions **1**

Library Instruction Type

7. Which of the following describe the types of formal library instruction provided to first year students at your institution: (Please check all that apply)
    d. **129**___One-class course related library instruction session
    e. **55**____One-class non-course related library instruction session (e.g. workshops)
    f. **85**___Guided Tour
    g. **29**___Web based virtual library tour
    h. **3**___Audio library tour
    i. **53**___Multiple sessions (e.g. 3 or more class sessions) course related instruction but not a separate credit course
    j. **6**___Required credit course taught by a librarian
    k. **11**___Elective credit course taught by a librarian
    l. **0**___Required credit course team taught by a librarian and a faculty member
    m. **0**___Elective credit course team taught by a librarian and a faculty member
    n. **0**___No formal library instruction is offered

*Please take these statistics from your most recent Academic Library Survey (ALS), formerly the IPEDS report, if possible.

> **Please submit course syllabi for credit-bearing library instruction courses for first year students at your institution.**

Competencies and skill objectives for first year students

8. Does your library and/or institution have a written statement of competencies and/or skill objectives for library instruction for first year students? (*153 responses*)
    - o. **51** Yes *33%*
    - p. **102** No 67%

> **Please submit documents or URL's which describe your student competency and/or skill objectives for first year students. Please include background information such as date of last revision, author(s), etc.**

9. Are library/research skills an articulated objective or competency in a required first year Student course at your institution? (*153 responses*)
    - a **71** Yes (please list specific classes or programs)
    - b **61** No (please explain)
    - q. **21** Don't know

Library Instruction Teaching Methods

10. Which of the following describe the types of assignments/projects designed for first year students (by their either a faculty instructor or a librarian) as part of their library instruction (Please check all that apply):
    - a. **35** Scavenger hunt with topics assigned by librarian
    - b. **42** Scavenger hunt with topics assigned by teaching faculty
    - c. **108** Bibliography or resource list in preparation for a paper, presentation, etc.
    - d. **24** Search logs or diaries
    - e. **71** Annotated list of sources
    - f. **19** Workbooks
    - g. **32** Online tutorials
    - h. _____ Other (please describe in detail)
    - i. **22** Exercises

> **Please submit documents or URLs describing prescribed assignments.**

> **Please submit documents or URL's describing any Online Tutorials you use with First Year Students. Please include background information such as author(s), date of last revisions, purpose, etc. (ex. This document was created in 2002 by a taskforce of 2 librarians and 2 faculty members, and we use it to supplement in-class instruction).**

11. At your institution, who is responsible for grading/evaluating student work done as part of a library session assignments? (Check as many as apply)
    a. __53__ Librarians
    b __79__ Faculty members
    c. __54__ Grading is not done

12. Which of the following describe the types of multi-media technology used in your instruction for first year students: (check all that apply)
    a. __83__ Powerpoint
    b. __7__ Listservs
    c. __9__ Chat Rooms
    d. __19__ Video (VHS or streaming)
    e. __133__ Projected demonstration of database
    f. __7__ Distance Instruction software (i.e. NetMeeting etc.)
    g. __16__ SmartBoards etc.
    h. __132__ Hands-on practice at a computer
    i. __58__ Web page designed for the class
    j. __29__ Course management software

13. What is the student class size that occurs most frequently in your instruction sessions for first year students? (*152 responses*)
    a. __22__ 15 students or less
    b. __110__ 16-25 students
    c. __20__ More than 20

14. How are your library instruction sessions generally planned?
    a. __59__ Librarian devised the library curriculum
    b. __1__ Faculty devised the library curriculum
    c. __89__ Librarian and faculty collaborated on the library curriculum

15. If you offer instruction as part of a freshman seminar, how are these sessions generally taught? (*105 responses*)
    a. __62__ Librarian teaches with faculty member present as an observer
    b. __32__ Librarian teaches with faculty member participating
    c. __11__ Librarian teaches without faculty member present

16. If you offer multiple course-related instruction sessions for freshmen library instruction how are these generally taught? (71 *responses*)
    a. __30__ Librarian teaches with faculty member present as an observer
    b. __35__ Librarian teaches with faculty member participating
    c. __6__ Librarian teaches without faculty member present

17. In the space below, please describe your multi-session instruction session. Include but do not limit your description to: number of sessions, if the course is required or non-required, for credit or not for credit, and under what discipline the course falls. _____

_____

_____

_____

18. Please use the space below to comment on the strengths and weaknesses of your overall library instruction program for first year students. _____

_____

_____

_____

Documents:
Competencies

After completing Colloquium the student will be able to:

I.   UNDERSTAND THE WAY COLLECTIONS OF
       INFORMATION SOURCES ARE
       PHYSICALLY ORGANIZED AND ACCESSED.

     A. The student will locate major physical areas of the
library:
>   Reference room
>   Mennonite Historical Library
>   Periodicals center   Art
Gallery
>   Circulation area
>   Curriculum Library
>   Stack areas

     B. The student will locate the key service areas in the
       library: Reference Desk Circulation Desk
       Periodicals Circulation Area

     C. The student will follow the procedures for finding
       and borrowing library books and videos, locating
       periodicals, and using the reserve collection.

II. CONSTRUCT A SEARCH STRATEGY RELEVANT TO
THE INFORMATION NEED.

     A. The student will identify and state the major
       questions.

     B. The student will determine type of information and
       sources needed.

     C. The student will translate questions into subject
       headings and keywords.

     D. The student will be able to broaden and/or narrow a
       topic.

III. CARRY OUT A SEARCH STRATEGY USING LIBRARY
RESOURCES.

     A. The student will find information on a topic in
       appropriate background sources--using both general
       and subject encyclopedias.

     B. The student will locate book reviews.

     C. The student will locate biographical information
       using general sources and subject specialized
       sources.

D. The student will find periodical articles on a selected topic by using general and specialized databases.

E. The student will have a basic understanding of the on-line catalog and make effective use of it through appropriate access points such as author, title, subject, or keyword.

F. The student will know the basic elements of bibliographic form and be able to use style manuals in the field. The student will avoid plagiarism by properly documenting sources.

G. The student will recognize that librarians are a part of the library resources and that the library is a useful place for research as well as study.

H. The student will be introduced to interlibrary loan procedures and policies.

IV. THE STUDENT WILL BEGIN TO DEVELOP CRITICAL EVALUATION SKILLS.

A. The student will evaluate the information retrieved whether in print or electronically, whether in a database or on a web site, discerning the strength and limitations of sources and their usefulness in relation to a selected topic.
    1. The student will be able to distinguish between scholarly and popular treatment of a topic.
    2. The student will be able to determine relevance of citations to research topics.
    3. The student will be aware of issues regarding currency, accuracy, bias, and controversy of a topic.

B. The students will decide if information needs have been adequately met and understand other options available.

Lafayette College Libraries Instruction Program
Mission Statement

The library instruction program supports the academic mission and curriculum of Lafayette College by means of course-integrated library instruction sessions. The aim of the program is to provide students with library research skills necessary to attain their academic goals and prepare them for lifelong learning in a society where information is organized in increasingly complex ways. Lafayette librarians seek a partnership with teaching faculty in creating a productive learning environment in which all students develop library research skills.

The structured instruction program has two core levels, one which reaches all first-year students through the First-Year Seminar and a second level designed for specialized or advanced coursework in majors and minors. As a complement to the structured program, librarians provide instruction during personalized reference appointments ("PRAs") with students.

I. First Level Library Instruction Goals for First-Year Seminars

All first-year students will be introduced to Lafayette Libraries and their basic resources, develop an understanding of how scholarly information is organized and retrieved, learn how to evaluate Web sites as tools for academic library research, and learn strategies for managing the library research process. These goals will be accomplished in a minimum of two class periods.

Introduction to Libraries
Students will learn the following:
1. How to navigate the library Web site.
2. How to use the library catalog and a basic periodical index (Expanded Academic Index) to find references to books and articles on a topic.
3. How to physically locate books and periodicals (Skillman, Kirby, Interlibrary Loan).
4. That librarians are available for assistance at all points in the research process.

Using the Web
Students will learn the following:
1. The nature of the World Wide Web (does not contain all information; unorganized; lacks editorial process).
2. How to evaluate Web sites for authority, accuracy, currency, and usability.
3. How to cite Web documents.

Additional goals for 100 Level Courses:

Basic concepts in information organization and retrieval
Students will learn the following:
1. How the purpose and characteristics of scholarly literature differ from general interest literature.

2. How libraries are institutions containing formats for storing knowledge that have evolved over time.

3. That most databases follow a common structure that can be exploited by various means to retrieve information, e.g., controlled vocabulary, keyword searching, Boolean operators.

Managing the library research process
Students will learn the following:
1. How to articulate a question, then limit or expand its scope.
2. How the scope of a project affects the types of sources used.
3. That the library research process is recursive and an understanding of the process can make for more productive searching.
4. That librarians are available for personalized research appointments.

II.   Second Level Library Instruction Goals

Students working in their major or minor will be introduced to specialized resources in a field of study, gain advanced understanding of the scholarly communication process, and learn additional strategies for using the World Wide Web as a research tool.

Introduction to specialized resources
Students will learn the following:
1 . How to identify and use major indexing tools in a field.
2. How to apply advanced search techniques for using indexes, e.g., proximity operators, and truncation.
3. How to use government documents, electronic journals, rare or archival material, or major scholarly Web sites.
4. How to use bibliographic information to evaluate the potential usefulness of a source.
5. How to acquire materials not at Lafayette.

Scholarly communication
Students will learn the following:
1. How new information is produced, reviewed, and disseminated in a field.
2. How certain factors affect the value of information in a field, e.g., author's credentials, publisher's reputation, number of times cited in literature.
3. How "primary sources" are defined in a field and why scholars use them.
4. What constitutes ethical use of scholarly resources.

Using the Web for research
Students will learn the following:
1. How Web sites are structured, e.g., internal vs. external links, URLs, and file names.
2. How search engines and directories work and their shortcomings.
3. How to find Web sites of organizations most likely to provide reliable information in a field.
4. That economic, ethical, and legal issues affect the presentation of information on Web sites.

Information Literacy Scoring Rubric - Level I

A. Recognize the need for information to clarify issues and support conclusions and judgements.
   - ❑ Participates in classroom discussion, conferences with faculty on research topics (assignments).
   - ❑ Gains familiarity with topic through general information sources (encyclopedias).
   - ❑ Develops a thesis statement.

B. Identify and retrieve relevant information from resources in different formats including technological ones as appropriate to a variety of resources.
   - ❑ Uses library catalog and indexes to identify information resources.
   - ❑ Retrieves supporting information from a variety of resources.

C. Evaluate the applicability on accuracy of information retrieved.
   - ❑ Selects the main ideas from the text.
   - ❑ Identifies popular and scholarly resources
   - ❑ Identifies primary and secondary sources.
   - ❑ Demonstrates understanding of possible biases in retrieved texts.
   - ❑ Reviews sources used and information retrieved and expands search if information need is not fully met.

D. Comply with the ethical and legal practices of information retrieval and use.
   - ❑ Demonstrates proper form for quoting verbatim material.
   - ❑ Restates textual concepts in his/her own words.
   - ❑ Uses an appropriate documentation style.

E. Demonstrate effective use of information technologies.
   - ❑ Uses class related information exchanges.
   - ❑ Accesses the online library catalog.
   - ❑ Uses electronic periodical indexes.
   - ❑ Uses electronic information databases as appropriate (examples: gov sites, CIAO, Issues & Controversies).
   - ❑ Uses electronic information directories to locate online information resources (examples: Librarians Internet Inventory, Infomine, and Internet Public Library).
   - ❑ Creates a product using a range of information technology (word-processing, spreadsheets, electronic slide shows, and Web pages) in a style that supports the product's primary message.

Messiah College

About Murray Library
Hours
Loan Policies
Staff
Community Users Info
Library Instruction
Information Literacy
First Year Students
Liaison Program

Library Guides
Reference
Acquisitions
Media Services
Friends of the Library

Online Resources
Murray Catalog
Area Colleges Catalog
Interlibrary Loan Forms
ProQuest
FirstSearch
Search the Web

Library Home Page
Messiah Home Page

First Year General Education _____
Approaches to Information Literacy

This component of *Approaches to Information Literacy* provides students with an introduction to basic skills in information retrieval, evaluation, and use. Further development of the abilities emphasized in this area is expected throughout the curriculum.

Objectives

After completing First Year Seminar, students will:

1. Know the location and function of essential areas in the library (Information and Circulation Desk; online catalog; reference collection; periodicals; stacks; and Media Services.
2. Know how to locate and check out library materials.
3. Understand that materials not owned by the library can be obtained from other sources.
4. Be able to focus and articulate their information need; and identify key concepts of their topic.
5. Understand the difference between controlled vocabulary (subject headings of descriptors assigned by the producer of an index or database) and key words.
6. Use key concepts to find resources on a topic by using the online catalog, periodical indexes and other sources as needed.
7. Interpret bibliographic citations from the search results and locate the materials cited.
8. Evaluate the information retrieved, discerning the strengths, limitations and usefulness in relation to a topic.
9. Incorporate retrieved information into their own texts.

First Year Seminar Library Competencies
Murray Library - Messiah College

A requirement for First Year Seminar is to achieve 80% on a short on-line test on material covered in the library instruction sessions. **Make sure I cover all these points by the end of the second session and that you understand them!**

Session I

Role of librarians in research

Library home page as gateway: What's available via the home page? [www.messiah.edu/library]

Access to resources beyond Murray Library
    -interlibrary loan

    -catalog for other libraries (consortium)

Library of Congress classification system

Murray Library Online Catalog: What's in it?

How to find Reserve books and their call numbers

Choosing and searching by keywords
    -looking at Subjects

Boolean operators:

    AND _____

    OR _____

Terminology:

    periodical

    keyword

    subject

Messiah College

<u>**Session II**</u>

Terminology:

Periodical index

Abstract

Citation

Arrangement of Murray Library periodicals

Selecting appropriate databases/indexes

Search by Topic [link on Lib. Home page: <u>htlp://www.messiah.edu/library/</u>

Proquest

Features most online databases have in common:

Reading bibliographic *citations* accurately

Citing a full-text article

NOTE: This is the outline given to First Year Seminar *students*.
Approved list of competencies is found on http://www.messiah.edu/library/first_year.html

North Central College Library Services
Information Literacy Program
2002-2003

Goals

The goals of the North Central College Library Services Information Literacy Program for students are the Information Literacy Competency Standards for Higher Education endorsed by the Association of College and Research Libraries (ACRL):

1. The information literate student determines the nature and extent of the information needed.
2. The information literate student accesses needed information effectively and efficiently.
3. The information literate student evaluates information and its sources critically and incorporates selected information into his or her knowledge base and value system.
4. The information literate student, individually or as a member of a group, uses information effectively to accomplish a specific purpose.
5. The information literate student understands many of the economic, legal, and social issues surrounding the use of information and accesses and uses information ethically and legally.

Orientations

General Oesterle Library orientation sessions are offered the second week of every term on Tuesday, 5:30-6:15pm and Saturday, 12:15-1:00pm. No prior sign-up is required. These sessions, taught by a librarian, introduce students (who have not attended a library instruction class or new student orientation) to methods of accessing both physical and online information in Oesterle Library. Participants will learn where resources are located within the library and how to use the Library Services Website, including the online information it provides.

Orientation sessions for specific groups of new students are held during campus orientation programs. These groups may include: all freshmen, graduate students, continuing education and transfer students, and special cohort groups. Usually taught by librarians in collaboration with the Information Technology Services (ITS) staff, these sessions include an introduction to the Library Services Website and library tour. (Hands-on searching exercises may also be included.)

Freshman Sequence

The cornerstone of the Information Literacy Program is the freshman English library instruction sequence, consisting of four phases for English 115 -116 (an online tutorial, one library instruction session in English 115 and two visits in English 116) and three phases for English 125 (an online tutorial and two library instruction sessions). Every freshman is expected to complete all phases in order, since each phase introduces new material and builds on the previous phases.

North Central College

Classes

In keeping with its commitment to information literacy, North Central College librarians encourage faculty to arrange for library instruction sessions for their courses. These sessions are designed to meet the needs of each course while encouraging students to grow as information literate individuals.

Library liaisons provide subject-specific library instruction addressing the needs of a specific assignment or course of study. These sessions may include instruction in the use of subject specific databases, such as ERIC, PsycINFO, or Synergy; the use of specialized reference sources; or any other material the instructor and library liaison feel is appropriate. During these sessions students refine the research skills they developed in the freshman English sequence. Sessions may be scheduled for all or part of a class period, and may be given by the library liaison in the classroom of the course or the classroom in the library (Class of 1997 Instruction Lab). The library requests that appointments for library instruction sessions be made at least one week prior to the requested date. Please contact your department or division's library liaison for further information.

NCC 120: Information Literacy and Research NCC 120: Information Literacy and Research is a 1.5 credit hour course offered the last five weeks of Winter Term. Focusing on the development of information literacy competencies, students completing this course will be able to locate, critically evaluate, and apply information that is appropriate to their specific needs. Contact the Instructional Services Librarian at 637-5707 for more information.

NORTH CENTRAL COLLEGE LIBRARY SERVICES
Information Literacy Program - Freshman Sequence 2002-2003

The goals of the North Central College Library Services Information Literacy Program for students are the Information Literacy Competency Standards for Higher Education endorsed by the Association of College and Research Libraries (ACRL). See attached.

Freshman English Instruction

The cornerstone of the Information Literacy Program is the freshman English library instruction sequence. Because the focus of the program is on enabling students to learn each information literacy concept well, the phases for 2001-2002 will be sequentially structured. One or two skills will be covered in depth each time the students meet with the Instructional Services Librarian, so that by the end of the year students will have mastered the following ACRL Standards Performance Indicators:

1. 1b   To develop a thesis statement and formulate the questions based on the information needed.
2. 2.b   To identify keywords, synonyms and related terms for the information needed.
2.2.c   To select controlled vocabulary specific to the discipline or information retrieval source.
2.2.d   To construct a search strategy using appropriate commands for the information retrieval system selected.
3.2.a   To examine and compare information from various sources in order to evaluate reliability, validity, accuracy, authority, timeliness, and point of view or bias.

The freshman English sequence of the Information Literacy Program consists of four phases for English 115-116 and three phases for English 125. It is essential that every freshman complete all phases in order, since each phase introduces new material and builds on the previous phase(s). Learning outcomes for each phase of the freshman English sequence for English 115 and 116 are:

English 115 - An Introduction to Information Literacy

Phase One:
Goal - To give students a basic introduction to North Central College's information resources.

Outcomes - Online Tutorial
Students will be able to:
1. Use the North Central College Library Services Web Site as a gateway to information.
2. Recognize the Dewey Decimal System.
3. Locate materials in Oesterle Library.
4. Locate an overview article on their topic by using the Reference Collection.
5. Search for a book or video using ILLINET Online.
6 Search for articles using an online database.
7. Use the Internet Resources section of the library web site as a gateway to information on the Web.

North Central College

Student Assessment
Students will be evaluated by the Instructional Services Librarian on:
1. The accuracy of their responses on the online tutorial worksheet.
2. The relevance to their stated topic of the resources selected on the online tutorial worksheet.

Phase Two:
Goals
1. To guide students in developing a focused, clear thesis statement/research question and to select appropriate search terms from that statement.
2. To guide students in understanding the content and construction of databases.
3. To guide students in locating periodical articles and books on their topic using the basic search function of bibliographic databases.

Outcomes - Library Instruction Session
Students will be able to:
1. State their research need in the form of a thesis statement or research question.
2. Identify all terms that could be used as key words in searching for information on this topic.
3. Suggest at least one possible term that might serve as a subject heading for this topic.
4. Select the most appropriate database(s) for their topic.
5. Search for articles and/or books, using appropriate online databases.
6. Select those articles and/or books that are most relevant to their topic in content and type.
7. Distinguish between articles available in full-text on the database they are searching, articles available in full-text on another database, articles available in paper or microform in Oesterle Library, and articles which can only be retrieved through interlibrary loan.

Student Assessment: Students will be evaluated:
1. By the Instructional Services Librarian on the quality of their participation in class exercises.
2. By their classroom instructor on the quality and relevance to their topic of the resources selected.

English 116 - Development of Information Literacy
Phase Three:
Goals
1. To guide students in refining their online search strategies.
2. To guide students in locating periodical articles and books on their topic using the advanced search function of bibliographic databases.
3. To enable students to distinguish between scholarly journals and popular magazines.
4. To introduce students to the concept of evaluating resources.

Outcomes
Students will be able to:
1. Locate at least one book or article using the advanced search function of a bibliographic database.
2. Distinguish between scholarly journals and popular magazines.
3. Evaluate all information gathered for appropriateness to their research question, credibility, currency, objectivity and accuracy.
4. Determine if the information gathered meets the need outlined.

Student Assessment Students will be evaluated:

1. By their classroom instructor on the quality and relevance to their topic of the resources chosen.
2. By the Instructional Services Librarian on the quality of their participation

Phase Four:
Goals

1. To guide students in locating academically reliable web sites relevant to their topic using a standard search engine and a scholarly web directory.
2. To guide students in evaluating the content of the web sites selected.

Outcomes - Library Instruction Session
Students will be able to:

1. Perform a focused search on a standard search engine and on a scholarly web directory.
2. Evaluate the information retrieved from the World Wide Web.
3. Determine if the information gathered meets the need outlined.

Student Assessment

1. By the Instructional Services Librarian on their written responses to two questions designed to reflect their grasp of the material presented.
2. By their classroom instructor on the quality and relevance of the web sites chosen.

English 125 - Development of Information Literacy
Phase One:

Goal - To give students a basic introduction to North Central College's information resources.

Outcomes - Online Tutorial
Students will learn to:

1. Use the North Central College Library Services Web Site as a gateway to information.
2. Recognize the Dewey Decimal System.
3. Locate materials in Oesterle Library.
4. Locate an overview article on their topic by using the Reference Collection.
5. Search for a book or video using ILLINET Online.
6. Search for articles using an online database.
7. Use the Internet Resources section of the library web site as a gateway to information on the Web.

Student Assessment
Students will be evaluated by the Instructional Services Librarian on:

1. The accuracy of their responses on the online tutorial worksheet.
2. The relevance to their stated topic of the resources selected on the online tutorial worksheet.

Phase Two:
Goals

1. To guide students in developing a focused, clear thesis statement/research question and to select appropriate search terms from that statement.
2. To guide students in developing an understanding of the content and use of bibliographic databases.

3. To guide students in locating periodical articles and books on their topic using the basic search function of bibliographic databases.

Outcomes
Students will be able to:
1 . State their research need in the form of a thesis statement or research question.
2. Identify all terms that could be used as key words in searching for information on this topic, and suggest at least one possible term that might serve as a subject heading for this topic.
3. Select the most appropriate database(s) for their topic.
4. Locate at least one book and/or article appropriate to their topic using the basic search function of a bibliographic database.
5. Select the book and/or article that is most relevant to their topic in content and type.
6. Distinguish between articles available in full-text on the database they are searching, articles available in full-text on another database, articles available in paper or Microform in Oesterle Library, and articles which can only be retrieved through interlibrary loan.

Assessment: Students will be evaluated:
1. By the Instructional Services Librarian on the quality of their participation in class exercises.
2. By their classroom instructor on the quality and relevance to their topic of the resources elected.

Phase Three
Goals
1 . To guide students in refining their online search strategies.
2. To guide students in locating periodical articles and books on their topic using the advanced search function of bibliographic databases.
3. To enable students to distinguish between scholarly j ournals and popular magazines.
4. To guide students in locating academically reliable web sites relevant to their topic.
5. To guide students in evaluating the resources retrieved.

Outcomes Students will be able to:
1. Locate at least one book or article using the advanced search function of a bibliographic database.
2. Perform a focused World Wide Web search.
3. Evaluate all information gathered for appropriateness to their research question, credibility, currency, objectivity and accuracy.
4. Determine if the information gathered meets the need outlined.

Assessment Students will be evaluated:
1. By their classroom instructor on the quality and relevance to their topic of the resources chosen.
2. By the Instructional Services Librarian on the quality of their participation in class exercises.

Program Assessment

English 115, 116 and 125 faculty will be asked to administer a brief (approximately ten short answer questions), anonymous assessment survey near the end of each academic term. The questions are designed to measure student learning over the course of the freshman English segment of the Information Literacy Program. Surveys are returned to the Instructional Services Librarian for grading and tabulation. Results will be used to modify the Information Literacy Program to address overall areas of weakness.

Library Research Competencies for Reed College Students

During the course of their years at Reed, students should advance beyond basic library skills, eventually gaining a broad understanding of the nature and organization of information resources and the ability to formulate and carry out library research in their chosen disciplines. The following list of competencies suggests appropriate levels of knowledge about library services and collections, as well as other information resources, to be acquired during successive stages of a Reed education.

Collectively, these competencies build toward an understanding of library research as a process. In order to reach a sufficient mastery of information resources to support thesis research, it is suggested that most research competencies be acquired prior to the senior year.

<u>**First Year Level Students Are Able to:**</u>
- use the library's course reserve system
- locate and use the library's collections and services
- distinguish between primary texts and critical works
- identify books and journal articles using catalogs, indexes, and other bibliographic databases
- interpret and use citations found in indexes, databases, notes, or bibliographies to locate books and journal articles in the Reed College Library
- locate and use dictionaries, subject encyclopedias, and reference materials
- locate and use nonprint resources
- locate and critically evaluate materials on the World Wide Web

<u>**Sophomore /Junior Level Students Are Able to:**</u>
- understand the nature of information resources in their major disciplines
- understand reference resources, including databases, indexes, and bibliographies, in their major disciplines
- locate and obtain books and journal articles from other libraries by borrowing directly and by using Orbis and interlibrary loan services
- locate and critically evaluate nonscholarly resources, such as current or contemporary news accounts
- locate and critically evaluate primary resources specific to the discipline, such as images, sound recordings, statistical data, or court decisions
- e-mail or download citations, text, and/or data from electronic resources and edit or manage this information using appropriate computer applications
- track information resources used in the course of their research and create accurate notes and bibliographies according to a style manual appropriate to the discipline
- understand issues relating to the ethical use of information, including concepts of intellectual property and copyright

<u>**Senior/Thesis Level Students Are Able to:**</u>
- understand specialized reference resources, including databases, indexes, and bibliographies, in support of thesis research
- locate, obtain, and critically evaluate information resources to support thesis research
- format the thesis according to Reed College requirements and appropriate style manuals

INFORMATION LITERACY

At Seton Hill University, one of our goals is to achieve information literacy for all students. This is accomplished by conducting at least two sessions of information literacy instruction for first-year students. The library staff coordinates with the faculty of the Seminar in Thinking and Writing in scheduling the sessions.

Seminar in Thinking and Writing focuses on writing, with inclusion of the related processes of critical reading, critical thinking, and oral communication. To assist in this learning experience, students are given information literacy instruction. An information literate student will be able to identify, locate, evaluate, extract, and employ information.

These competencies are defined as:

1. Identify - The student will be able to identify a source as popular culture, news, or scholarly through discernment of its characteristics.

2. Locate - The student will know how to use the online resources at Seton Hill University to find the information he/she needs.

3. Evaluate - The student will be able to examine a source and determine its worth in relation to his/her particular need.

4. Extract - The student will know how to extract the information so that it is useful to him/her within the context of the particular project being researched.

5. Employ - The student will know how to cite the information and use it so that it serves its intended purpose in the research process.

These competencies will be developed through these methods: verbal instructions, hands-on identification practice, searching demonstrations, online catalog and database training and practice, worksheets, online tutorials (currently under construction), and hand-outs. Follow-up will take place with the faculty, and problem areas will be discussed.

All students receive formal library instruction in <u>English 111</u>, <u>English 112</u>, and <u>Senior Seminar</u> sessions.

English 111 Library Orientation for Information Literacy

The library session is intended to introduce students to the library facility and services.

The session is conducted in the library in a space with a computer and computer projector. The librarian demonstrates the library website, specifically the local catalog and elements in a catalog record, OhioLINK central catalog and elements in a central catalog record including the loan request option, Library of Congress Subject Headings, and several OhioLINK full-text research databases. Several of the OhioLINK research databases have different user interface features. There is a brief tour of the library and review of the stack locations.

Information literacy is the ability to access, evaluate, and use information from a variety of sources. One indicator includes "The information literate student identifies a variety of types and formats of potential sources for information."

The instructional objectives - students will have the ability to:

- identify library hours of operation
- identify library locations, circulating stacks, special locations, and study stations, etc.
- identify and use circulation services, e.g. borrowers card, reserve collection and options for returning materials
- use the Library of Congress classification system and subject headings
- use the electronic card catalog (OPAC) - SSU local and OhioLINK central
- use the electronic research databases, fulltext encyclopedias and dictionaries
- identify the arrangement of books, documents, current periodicals, microformats and public computers

Following the tour the students are given the opportunity to complete a Library exercise sheet:

- to demonstrate the ability to list information from a catalog record as found on the SSU local library catalog
- to retrieve an item from the library shelves using the call number
- to use the OhioLINK central catalog and identify a subject(s) on a catalog record
- to use the Library of Congress Subject Headings, LCSH, to trace a subject
- to demonstrate the use of fulltext databases and identify author and references for an entry
- to interact with library staff for questions and assistance

The exercise sheet is designed so students can have their work checked by the library reference staff and be given the opportunity to ask questions about the process. They will have an opportunity to know librarians and library staff are a HELPFUL resource. Handouts include the library guide, outline of the Library of Congress classification schedule and exercise sheet.

English 112 Bibliographic Instruction for Information Literacy

This 90-minute information literacy orientation is given during one class meeting for students in English 112. This orientation takes place in an English computer lab so each student simulates online searches. It is designed to introduce all students to a systematic search process for identifying and gathering information for a research paper. Information literacy skills are interdisciplinary and can be used for all assignments in a subject.

INFORMATION LITERACY STANDARD: The information literate student accesses needed information effectively and efficiently. One indicator includes "The information literate student retrieves information online or in person using a variety of methods."

The instructional objectives - students will:

- choose and narrow a topic (argumentative)
- identify background information (overview)
- review the SSU local and OhioLINK central catalogs to identify classified items
- select and use electronic periodical indexes (subject-specific)
- identify resources to evaluate the information retrieved
- use OhioLINK loan and interlibrary loan for items not in the SSU collection

The format for this orientation is a demonstration/hands-on session given in the English computer lab. The search process is briefly explained and librarians show students actual samples of the various electronic resources available for use. The hand-out is a diagram of the steps to follow to identify information, a bibliography of a selective list of reference titles in the SSU library collection, an overview of periodical types, a list of suggestions for evaluating resources, brief explanations of the SSU library and OHIOLINK services and internet access options.

The orientations are scheduled during the first three weeks of the quarter or when the assignment for writing the research paper is given.

Librarians focus on SSU students' broad educational needs in all disciplines taught in the academic curriculum. This orientation is one segment to prepare students in all the SSU academic programs to access information systematically and successfully.

Senior Seminar Information Literacy Orientation

The library orientation is intended to demonstrate the research strategy for identifying information students will need for their paper and oral presentation. The session is conducted in a computer lab and all students are guided through a sample search using the library webpage. The session takes about 2 hours and is more meaningful if the teaching faculty assists the librarians. Faculty who participate, interject comments, and ask questions promote more successful sessions.

Information literacy performance indicator includes, "The information literate student extracts, records, and manages the information and its sources."

Advanced search techniques are demonstrated.

The instructional objectives - students will:

- Identify a variety of types and formats of potential sources for information
- Select the most appropriate investigative methods or information retrieval systems for accessing the needed information
- Construct and implement effectively designed search strategies
- Retrieve information online or in person using a variety of methods
- Refine the search strategy if necessary
- Extract, record, and manage the information and its sources

This session will help students to plan a flexible research strategy and recognize the tools to locate information.

Database searching proficiency will include:

- Conduct a search query using *Boolean logic and truncation*
- Use the online public access catalogs and research database *limit features*
- Use the OhioLINK loan option
- Use the Table of Contents option
- Use the *export and downloading features*
- Review *controlled vocabulary* and *Library of Congress subject headings*
- Evaluate the information for relevance, authoritativeness, and appropriateness

Other objectives include students should have the ability to

- Keep a working bibliography
- Use the librarians as resources and schedule a research consultation
- Be familiar with the Critical Reasoning Rubric and Writing Rubric used in evaluating their research process

Available online at: http://www.shawnee.edu/offices/clarklib/clarklibinfo/libinstruction.htm

Proposal for Library and Information Skills Workshops

Rationale for Teaching Library and Information Skills to First Year Students

First year students have never come to the University of Richmond with adequate skills in using the resources of a college library, but until recently most of them knew how to use a catalog to find a book and how to use an index to find an article in a journal. This is no longer the case. Increasing numbers of students have never used anything but the Internet to find information and do not understand why anyone would bother using anything else. They have no conception of scholarship and the role it plays in their education. Until they do, they cannot understand why one source of information might be preferable to another, still less to see themselves as scholars.

In meetings and focus groups, students who have reached more advanced levels indicate that they would like to improve their knowledge of library resources and wish they had known more early in their academic careers. Members of a faculty focus group have also said that they wanted students, including those in general education courses, to understand how research is conducted and results reported in their fields. But students who cannot find an article in a scholarly source or distinguish it from a web page published by a special interest group will hardly be able to understand the nature of an academic discipline and its intellectual protocols.

The online Library and Information Skills Tutorial (LIST), a prerequisite for these workshops, is a basic orientation to the library and its resources, but does not allow for active questioning, hands-on practice, and personal feedback. These workshops are intended to fill that gap by having the students not only learn to search the catalog and other databases, but also to evaluate sources of information, to physically retrieve materials, and to comprehend the relationship between a citation and its associated document. The goal is both to equip students with the basics skills needed for course-related research assignments and to help them recognize that the library's resources can help them answer many of the questions that arise as they prepare for and participate in classes. The workshops are not designed to replace discipline specific instruction for upper level courses.

Library Research & Information Skills Competencies

Basic Competencies

Students should:

- Understand that materials in academic libraries are classified by subject and be able to interpret a call number.

- Be able to identify the parts of a bibliographic record.

- Be able to use reference tools such as dictionaries, encyclopedias, handbooks, almanacs, and statistical sources to focus a research question.

- Be able to distill a complicated research question into searchable concepts/keywords/synonyms.

- Understand the concept and usefulness of a controlled vocabulary (all online catalogs and many databases and indexes use controlled vocabularies).

- Understand the difference between subject searching and word searching.

- Understand search features of the online catalog and online indexes/databases (Boolean, truncation, etc.).

- Be able to formulate a research strategy, and understand the process through which questions are refined, and redefined in the course of research.

- Understand that both popular and scholarly material exists on most any topic; be able to distinguish between these two types of material, and determine when it is appropriate to use each type and why.

- Be able to distinguish between primary and secondary resources; be able to determine when it is appropriate to use these two types of resource and why.

- Understand the nature of periodical literature, and why and when it is useful.

- Understand what periodical literature abstracts and indexes do, and why they are useful. Understand that these resources vary in scope (what subjects are included, how many titles are indexed, etc.), arrangement (classified, subject, etc.), and content (full-text, abstracts, citation only).

- Be able to critically evaluate information for usefulness, bias, currency and authority (including Internet resources).

- Have an understanding of plagiarism and intellectual property issues -- quoting, paraphrasing, attributing ideas; what is fair use?

- Be able to use a style manual to correctly document information sources in different formats.

- Select appropriate technologies for the presentation of information gathered (i.e. graphical presentation software, word processing, HTML editor, statistical software).

Advanced Competencies

Students should:

- Be familiar with the subject-specific tools in their discipline (indexes, abstracts, electronic texts, and other specialized resources).

- Understand how scholars and practicing professionals in their discipline generate, control, and use information (published/unpublished sources, electronic & personal communications, etc.).

- Understand and effectively communicate the steps required for effective research, including formulating a thesis, creating a search strategy, and using a variety of sources.

- Develop the ability to critique their own research process; was the original need met? Or did the goal change?

- Synthesize main ideas; construct new concepts; compare new and prior knowledge; assess new knowledge against existing knowledge.

Available at:
http://oncampus.richmond.edu/is/library/social_sciences.compencies.html

Wartburg College

Information Literacy
Across the Curriculum (ILAC) Plan

October 9, 2002

Below are five classes that every Wartburg student must take under the Essential Education plan. There are two goals:

1. To cover the National Competency Standards for Information Literacy as recommended in 2000 by the Association of College Research Libraries (ACRL), and

2. To teach the standards in a way that does not duplicate other lessons and is instructive to a variety of learning styles.

Foundational Class	ILAC lesson covered
IS 101	Choosing relevant search terms that lead to good retrieval. Students work with secondary sources to develop a basic understanding of the topic and a list of possible terms to use in further searching.
IS 201	(*second-year seminar entitled "Living in a Diverse World"*). Bias and perspective in information. Involves comparison of information from different disciplines, worldview of author, and/or close reading of a text to discover bias evident in subtle aspects of presentation.

Scientific Reasoning	(*students must choose one of six courses*). The differences between scholarly and popular information and how scientific achievement is translated for a lay audience. Requires comparison of journal and newspaper articles.
EN 112	Search strategy and evaluation of information based on age and nature of source and credibility of author.
RE 101	(*Literature of the Old and New Testament*). Specialized tools specific to Biblical studies, introducing the concept of the particular scholarly apparatus of different disciplines.

In addition, each department will design, in consultation with an Information Literacy Librarian (Randall Schroeder, Karen Lehmann, and Jill Gremmels) an ILAC strand for the department. All faculty can be assured that when a student finishes any of the above classes, librarians and faculty will have instructed them and have put to practice the Information Literacy concepts linked to the class.

Randall Schroeder
Information Literacy
Librarian
Wartburg College Vogel
Library

Karen Lehmann
Information Literacy
Librarian
Wartburg College Vogel
Library

Wartburg College Vogel Library
100 Wartburg Blvd.
PO Box 1003
Waverly, Iowa 50677
(319) 352-8477

Available at: http://www.wartburg.edu/library/infolit/ilac.,html

Western New England College

Western New England College
Information Literacy for First Year Students

Students at Western New England College will have an opportunity to work on a sequence of information literacy objectives during their first year. Four times during their first year, students will encounter concepts of information literacy in certain required courses in collaboration with D'Amour Library's Information Literacy Program. The sequence of classes includes First Year Seminar, English Composition I, Health (PEHR IS 1), English Composition II.

Objectives & Outcomes:

First Year Seminar:

1. Students will be able to identify the steps of the information research process.
2. Students will to able to discuss the role of information research in the process of learning and creating.
3. Students will be able to identify the different information tools available for research.
4. Students will be able to select resources in order to access appropriate sources for any given informational need.
5. Students will be able to construct simple search strategies.
6. Students will be able to employ the use of synonyms to make a search more comprehensive.
7. Students will be able to identify the difference between popular and scholarly articles.

Health Class:

1. Students will be able to identify reliable health related specialized encyclopedias and reference resources.
2. Students will be able to select an appropriate database resource in order to access health related articles.
3. Students will be able to construct a basic subject search using the subject thesaurus.
4. Students will be able to locate a reliable health article on a specific topic.

English Composition I:

1. Students will be able to evaluate information sources in order to determine scope, authority, credibility, validity, audience and timeliness.
2. Students will be able to recognize instances of plagiarism.
3. Students will be able to construct bibliographic citations in the correct format while protecting academic integrity.

English Composition II:

1. Students will be able to identify appropriate resources to find critical information on a literary topic.
2. Students will be able to integrate their thoughts with published research into a paper.
3. Students will know the difference between author, title, keyword and subject searching.

Suggested Content
First Year Seminar:

- Students complete Introduction and Module I of TILT, an on-line tutorial developed at the University of Texas (http://tilt.lib.utsystem.edul). The quiz at the end of Module I should be taken and the results printed so that completion can be verified. Outcomes of TILT include the following:
    - Identify a variety of information sources
    - Recognize that appropriate sources of information will change depending on need
    - Identify characteristics of information on the Web
    - Identify characteristics of library resources
    - Recognize that library collections are located beyond the Web
    - Recall what you would find in a periodical index
    - List reasons to use a periodical index
    - Distinguish between popular and scholarly periodicals

- Students attend a class in the D'Amour Library with a Research Instruction Librarian (preferably during the month of September or early October)
    - Students will recall role and importance of the body of recorded knowledge in learning as discussed in "Creating Minds" by Howard Gardner
    - Librarian will introduce databases available from library homepage to access information
        - Online catalog, reference, and one database
    - Librarian will introduce searching techniques
        - Keyword
        - Subject
    - Librarian will introduce Boolean logic
        - Students will practice Boolean logic with physical exercise
    - Librarian will introduce use of synonyms
        - Students will brain storm synonyms for topic

    Students will complete Module 2 along with quiz of TILT as homework after Information Research instruction. http://tilt.lib.utsystem.edu/ Outcomes Include:
    - Identify appropriate strategies for selecting search terms
    - Identify types of information available in library databases
    - Select appropriate library databases
    - Identify common fields in a library database
    - List methods to search using keywords and subject headings
    - Combine search terms effectively
    - Describe information available from a search engine
    - Select appropriate strategies for searching the Web

Health:
- Students will have an assignment to find and read one authoritative article on a health topic.
- Students will brain storm about how one goes about finding popular and scholarly articles on health
- Librarian will introduce health reference books
- Discuss using reference resources for authoritative information
- Librarian will introduce General Health database; fee vs. free information
- Librarian will demonstrate subject search using subject guide and natural language searching.   Students will practice subject searching.

English Composition 1:
- Students will complete module 3 of TILT (http://tilt.lib.utsystem.edu/)
- Students will compare several web pages on same subject looking at authority, scope & purpose, credibility, validity, objectivity, and timeliness
  - (think, pair, share)
- Students will discuss different occurrences of plagiarism
  - Define elements of plagiarism
- Students will view examples of correct citations

English Composition II:
- Students review steps of research process
- Share results
- Librarian introduces research resources for literary criticism paper
- Students will review concepts of plagiarism
- Think, pair, share
- Students will discuss how their voice can be incorporated into research paper
- Knowledge pyramid

FIRST-YEAR SEMINAR LIBRARY COMPONENT: BUILDING FOUNDATIONS

The library component of the First-Year Seminar provides the opportunity for students to begin to learn the research skills that are necessary in an academic environment and crucial to information literacy.

To ensure academic success for our students:

- Students should develop confidence in using a college library
- Students should be introduced to the Library as place, and as gateway to information on a networked campus
- Students should be aware of the role of librarians as resources and partners in learning
- Students should have opportunities to engage intellectually with a topic, controversies within that topic, and sources pertaining to them
- Students should have multiple opportunities to develop computer skills.

Students should begin to learn research skills crucial to information literacy:

- Formulate (clarify, revise, and refine) a research question
- Devise and implement an effective search strategy
- Learn effective use of ELIZA, Wheaton's online catalog
- Select and use an appropriate full-text journal database or periodical index, print or online, for a topic search, and interpret citations
- Learn how to gain access to books, periodicals, reference materials, videos, etc. in or from the Wallace Library, whatever the format
- Develop and apply initial criteria for evaluating information and its sources
- Acknowledge the use of information sources appropriately; cite in consistent manner.

Planning:

- Stimulating, carefully planned instructional sessions, including demonstration of and practice with selected sources, which culminate in a carefully wrought assignment, where students put new and important skills into practice is our shared goal.
- Clear, direct library component assignments which encourage the development of fundamental research skills in students are the most effective.
- Timing of library class(es) should be relative to the due date of the assignment, and to students' readiness to focus on research. *Be alert to the flood of new experiences early in the semester!*
- Successful library components are the result of serious, semester-long collaboration between faculty and librarian.

Last updated on 7/31/02

Available at: http://www.wheatoncollege.edu/Library/Reference/FYSgoals.html.

William Patterson College

Learning Objectives for User Education

Population	Student Learning Outcome Objectives	Freshman Seminar Suggestions
Freshman	*Core Concepts for Instruction:*	
	+Understand and identify the library services and personnel when necessary; able to approach staff for assistance.	+Describe library service philosophy and distribute Freshman orientation packet.
	+Identify Physical Components of the library - service points and major collection areas.	+Provide a tour of the facility: can be a "virtual tour" using the library's home page, map included in packet or suggest online tutorial.
	+Utilize the Library of Congress Classification system.	+Review of subject, call number and location handout.
	+Understand information contained in the library's online catalog: components of a record; how to search fields; ability to locate material.	+Overview of handout and live demonstration of search and display functions of the catalogue.
	+Construct a basic keyword search to retrieve materials in a general electronic database (e.g. Academic Search Premier, Wilson Omnifile).	+Describe basic components and functions of an electronic index entry (eg. citation, abstract, descriptors).
	Additional Concepts for discussion:	
	+Identify basic parameters of fair use of copyrighted materials, issues of plagiarism and documenting sources.	+Review citation format and citing documents handout.
	+Comprehend basic differences between scholarly and popular works in periodicals.	+Use of general database (Academic Search Premier/WilsonOmnifile) to demonstrate the organization, language and content differences.
	+Aware that remote access is provided to the library databases.	+Inform students about IT services and remote access handout.

Documents:
Course Syllabi

IDS100
InfoMania
Creating, Managing, and Seeking Information
in the 21st Century

Time / Place: 8:20 — 9:20 a.m. M W F, Library Electronic Classroom
Instructors: Geri Worley gworley@bsc.edu & Charlotte Ford cford@bsc.edu
Teaching Assistant: Kyndle Huey jkhuey@bsc.edu
Phones: 226-4741 & 226-4749
Office hours: Immediately following class (or by appointment)

Course description:

It is often said that we live in "the information age." What, exactly, does this mean? In this course, you will have an opportunity to construct your own answer to this question. We will experience the information life cycle (creation, dissemination, organization, and use of information) and explore the impact of current information technologies on the cycle and its participants. We will spend hands-on time mastering various tools and strategies for creating, locating, and using information. You will use these tools and techniques to develop an annotated bibliography on an appropriate topic of interest to you, and will have the chance to apply your technological skills to an information-related project in the community.

Course goals:

This 1Y course will provide a structure and a setting in which you can develop your communicative, collaborative, and technological skills. By the end of the semester, you should:

- Be a more proficient searcher, evaluator, and designer of information resources
- Have a general understanding of the history of information technology
- Understand some of the major information issues currently facing our society, and be able to articulate and substantiate your opinions on these issues
- Feel comfortable collaborating with and assisting others in the use of information technology

Course requirements:

- As a BSC student, you are expected to abide by the rules of the BSC Honor Code.
- You are expected to attend class regularly, complete assigned readings, and participate actively in class discussions.
- Assignments should be turned in on time; a percentage of the grade will be taken off for late assignments.
- The following texts are **required**:

➤ Jonscher, C. (2000). *The evolution of wired life: from the alphabet to the soul-catcher chip – how information technologies change our world.* New York: John Wiley & Sons.

➤ Baird, R.M., Ramsower, R., & Rosenbaum, S.E. (2000). *Cyberethics: social & moral issues in the computer age.* Amherst, N.Y.: Prometheus Books.

➤ Additional readings will be made available to you in digital format and/or placed on reserve in the library.

- One text is **recommended**: Lunsford, A.A. (2001). *The everyday writer* (2nd ed.). Boston & New York: Bedford / St. Martin's. This book will be used in your EH102 class; it is also available on a networked campus computer near you, and <u>on the Web</u> (**login required!**).

Assignments:

1. *Reflections on the readings*

   Thoughtful reading is essential to your success in this class. In most sessions for which there are readings assigned, you will prepare a brief reflection inspired by the reading. Each reflection must be submitted to the Blackboard digital drop box by 7:30 am on the day it is due.

2. *Exercises*

   Over the course of the term, you will complete a series of exercises that will enhance your ability to search, evaluate, and design information products. Some in-class time will be allotted for working on each of these exercises.

3. *Leading discussion on information issue*

   Early in the term, you will sign up (with one or two fellow students) to lead a discussion on one of the information issues, which we will begin to cover on October 8. As discussion leaders, you will be responsible for reviewing postings to Blackboard in advance and guiding the in-class discussion. This is a great chance to use your imagination: controversial questions, thought-provoking activities, and creative use of media are encouraged!

4. *Annotated bibliography*

For your term project, you will compile an annotated bibliography of resources on an information issue of your choice. This project will allow you to put to use many of the skills covered in class. Several steps are involved:

- o Identify a question involving information technology that is of interest to you.
- o Locate a variety of sources (including books, articles, and websites) that you believe would help you (or anyone else!) to explore this question.
- o Evaluate these sources: which are the most useful?
- o Cite and annotate the **best** sources, making sure to include a variety of formats.
- o Make the citations + annotations available in a Microsoft Access database.

More information on this project (including a list of possible topics and information on citing and annotating sources) will be handed out in class, and we will work on it together throughout the term. Some of the exercises we complete should also help you to compile your bibliography of sources. A brief description of the topic or question you are interested in exploring is due in class on **9/14**. On **10/17**, you will submit a brief progress report. The finished product will be presented in class at the end of the term.

5. *Community project*

In this time of rapid technological change, there are many options for community service. Several options will be offered in class. They may include introducing elementary school students to PowerPoint or web surfing; working with senior citizens who are interested in learning about online searching; making BSC publications available online; or helping BSC departments enhance their web presence. You are welcome to suggest a project of your own (*but please note*: instructor approval is required). You should plan to devote approximately 10 hours to this project, including time for planning, implementation, and reflection. The community project may be completed in a group or on an individual basis.

Evaluation & Grading:

Grades will be assigned according to the BSC Grading System

(A= Distinctive; B= Very good; C=Satisfactory; D=Lowest passing grade; F=Failure)

The following table summarizes assignments and their worth:

Birmingham Southern College

Assignment	% of grade	Due Date
Reflections on the readings (10)	20%	Most Mondays by 7:30 a.m.
Exercises (7)	25%	9/17, 9/24, 10/1, 10/8, 10/15, 11/5, 11/30
Annotated bibliography	35%	*Description*: due 9/14 *Progress report*: due 10/17 *Final bibliography*: due at final exam period
Community project	10%	As scheduled (reflection due by 12/7)
Class participation (including Blackboard & in-class participation, and leading discussion on an info issue)	10%	Throughout the term

Schedule of Readings & Assignments

*Please complete readings & assignments **before** class on the date listed, unless otherwise noted.*

Week 1: Introduction to the course, to Blackboard & Word, and to APA style

8/29	Post classmates' information to Blackboard (in class)
8/31	Log in to Blackboard and look in the "Classmates" folder (under Course Documents) Read prologue of *Evolution* Skim 52.c. APA style for a list of references in *The Everyday Writer*

Week 2: Key issues and history of information technology

9/3	Labor Day (**no class**)
9/5	Read & reflect *Evolution* chapter 1
9/7	Examine http://www.tcf.ua.edu/courses/Jbutler/T389/ITHistoryOutline.htm and http://photo2.si.edu/infoage/infoage.html

Week 3: History of info tech
Data, information & knowledge; the information life cycle; formats of information

9/10	Read & reflect *Evolution* chapter 2
9/12	Read *Research process* chapter 1 (1997 ed.) and pp.3-8 (2001 ed.) (on reserve)
9/14	Hand in proposed topic for annotated bibliography Exercise 1: Formats of info (due 9/17)

Week 4: The shift to electronic information; finding information in databases

9/17	Read & reflect *Evolution* chapters 3 & 4
9/19	Read *Research process* chapter 4 (on reserve)
9/21	Exercise 2: finding info in databases (due 9/24)

Week 5: Enter the Internet; finding information on the Web

9/24	Read & reflect *Evolution* chapter 6
9/26	Read *Research process* chapter 6 (on reserve) and Are our academic libraries ready for the Internet generation? (at http://www.educause.edu/ir/library/html/cem991a.html)
9/28	Consider: www.searchenginewatch.com Exercise 3: finding info on the Web (due 10/1)

Week 6: Evaluating information

10/1	Read & reflect *Evolution* chapter 5
10/3	Read Quality of information in *Digital Mythologies* (on reserve); read 12.b. Assess the usefulness of a source and 12.c. Evaluate electronic sources... in *The Everyday Writer*
10/5	Exercise 4: evaluating info (due 10/8)

Week 7: Issue: economics of information. Skill: PowerPoint

10/8	Read & reflect *Evolution* chapter 7
10/10	Read Absolute Powerpoint (on reserve)
10/12	Exercise 5: PowerPoint (due 10/15)

Week 8: Issue: anonymity & information technology. Skill: creating Web pages

10/15	Read & reflect *Cyberethics* Chapters 8 (Kling et al.) and 9 (Turkle)
10/17	Hand in progress report on annotated bibliography See links to Tutorials & Guides in Blackboard
10/19	Fall break (**no class**)

Weeks 9 & 10: Issue: privacy of information. Skill: creating Web pages (cont'd)

10/22	Read & reflect *Cyberethics* Chapters 11 (Schulman) and 12 (Wright & Kakalik)
10/24	See links to Tutorials & Guides in Blackboard
10/26	See links to Tutorials & Guides in Blackboard
10/29	See links to Tutorials & Guides in Blackboard
10/31	Exercise: Web pages (due 11/5)
11/2	Registration (**no class**)

Week 11: Issue: ownership of information. Skill: building databases

11/5	Read & reflect *Cyberethics* chapters 16 (Godwin) and 18 (DeLong)
11/7	See links to Tutorials & Guides in Blackboard
11/9	See links to Tutorials & Guides in Blackboard

Week 12: Issue: accessibility of information. Skill: building databases (cont'd)

11/12	Read & reflect Digitally empowered development (on reserve) and

	Libraries & the Internet (on reserve)
11/14	See links to Tutorials & Guides in Blackboard
11/16	See links to Tutorials & Guides in Blackboard

Weeks 13 & 14: Issue: online relationships & community. Skill: building databases (cont'd)

11/19	Read & reflect *Cyberethics* chapter 22 (Meeks) and 23 (Katz & Aspden)
11/21 11/23	Thanksgiving Break (**no class**)
11/26	Exercise: Databases (due 11/30)
11/28	Exercise: Databases (cont'd - due 11/30)

Weeks 14 & 15: Individual consultation on final projects; community service

11/30	Individual meetings / Community service
12/3	Individual meetings / Community service
12/5	Individual meetings / Community service Reflection on community service due by 12/7

Finals period

Final exam	Read *Evolution* chapter 9 & epilogue Present final projects

Available at: http://panther.bsc.edu/~libref/ids100.html

California State University, San Marcos
Library & Information Services

GEL 101 Library Module: Information and Society

INSTRUCTORS: Ann M. Fiegen, Business Librarian   **INSTRUCTORS:** Hua Yi, Social Sciences

Phone: 750-4365	Phone: 750-4368
Email: afiegen@csusm.edu	Email: hyi@csusm.edu
Office Hours: By appointment	Off ice Hours: By appointment
Office Location: CRA 3307	Office Location: CRA 4221 -B

MODULE DESCRIPTION

Students will learn the skills required to conduct research at a college level, which once mastered, will foster the ability to access, evaluate, and communicate information effectively. The module will introduce students to a variety of different research methods and information formats, which will help develop critical thinking skills and the creation of effective research strategies.

MODULE OBJECTIVES

1. Become familiar with the physical layout of the library as well as the types of library materials and services available.

2. Understand classification in an academic library and the usefulness of controlled vocabulary. Use and understand commands of the on-line catalog and be able to identify the parts of a record.

3. Gain knowledge of the types of subject-specific reference sources available and understand how to use them.

4. Learn to find an article using an index. Become familiar with the different formats of indexes available including print and electronic.

5. Become familiar with types of information available on the Internet; effectively use directories, indexes and various search engines. Identify characteristics of an authoritative website.

6. Be able to critically evaluate information for usefulness, bias, currency and authority.

7. Use a style manual to correctly document information sources in many different formats.

8. Understand and effectively communicate the steps required for effective research, including formulating a thesis, creating a search strategy using a variety of sources.

GRADING

There are six class sessions for this module worth a total of 90 points, You will have an activity in each class session. Be on time for class. Participate in class discussions. Complete all assignments on time, as outlined in the class schedule. Read assigned sections from your textbook.

PATHFINDER FORMAT AND GUIDELINES

TOPIC
A limited subject will work best. The topic should be typed in all capital letters and centered one and one-half inches from the top of the page (do not use the section heading "topic").

Example ,
CHILD ABUSE: THE GENERATION CYCLE

Introduction: Child abuse is the intentional harm (physical or emotional) to a child by a parent or guardian. When children who have been beaten grow up to abuse their own children, this is known as the generation cycle.

INTRODUCTION (2 points)
A concise explanatory, factual statement to define and delimit your topic. This note should be in your words.

ENCYCLOPEDIAS, DICTIONARIES, AND OTHER REFERENCE SOURCES (4 points total: 2 points for 2 reference works, and 2 points for the description of the works) Two relevant titles must be included. Briefly describe their relevance to your topic. You may wish to cite specific articles or suggest key terms defined in the reference works. Be sure to cite using the APA style for both reference works.

ACCESS TERMS FOR THE ONLINE CATALOG (4 points total: 2 for subject headings and 2 for Keyword terms) , Prioritize the best subject headings to look under in the online catalog. At least two subject headings should be included. In a separate column, list Keyword terms (not established subject headings) that can also be used to access materials in the Online Public Access Catalog. At least two terms should be included.

Example:
CHILD ABUSE
CHILD ABUSE -- CASE STUDIES
CRUELTY TO CHILDREN
CHILD WELFARE
CHILDREN -- LAW
CHILDREN'S RIGHTS

Additional Public Access Catalog Keyword Terms
CHILD NEGLECT
CHILD BEATING

BOOKS (3 points total: 1 for each book you find)
Three books from this campus library must be included. This does NOT include reference books. All three books should be cited using APA style.

INDEXES (4 points total: 2 points for 2 indexes you list and 2 points for two search statements) Two periodical indexes must be listed. Give the full title of the Index and list the actual search statement you used in each index. Least at least two search statements you used to search for articles.

ARTICLES (6 points total: 3 points for three articles and 3 points for annotating one scholarly article.)

Three articles must be included, one must be a scholarly article. Include your annotated paragraph for the scholarly article. List here periodical and newspaper articles on your topic that are particularly timely or informative. Be sure to cite using the APA style for all three articles.

INTERNET SOURCES AND OTHER MEDIA (3 points total: 1 point for the Internet site and 2 points for Web site evaluation) No more than one high quality Internet source. An Internet source that adds substantive additional information to your topic must be included here. Write one paragraph to evaluate your site applying Web site evaluation criteria. Be sure to cite using the APA style for electronic resources.

California State University, San Marcos

SUMMARIZING COMMENTS (2 points extra credit)
Discuss in a single paragraph problems a user might encounter when researching this topic. Points to consider include: more literature available on topic than can be used; very little available in books, journals, etc.; available information too peripheral; many of the sources in foreign languages, non-availability of sources on campus; general tips for an effective search.

GENERAL GUIDELINES

* The final copy of your pathfinder must be typed.
* Cite all entries according to the APA style manual. **(4 points will be credited to correct use of APA style: 1 for reference works, 1 for books, 1 for articles, and 1 for Internet site)**
* The section headings should be in all capitals.
* Arrange the entries in each section alphabetically.

USE THE FOLLOWING CRITERIA TO EVALUATE EACH SOURCE:
a) Relevancy to topic
b) Currency of information
c) Authority
d) Objectivity or viewpoint
e) Accuracy

Grading Rubric for the Research Guide: Total Points 30

Introduction	2 points
2 reference works	2 points
Description of reference work	2 points
2 Subject Headings	2 points
2 keyword search terms for books	2 points
3 books	3 points
2 periodical Indexes	2 points
2 search terms for articles	2 points
3 articles	3 points
Annotation of one scholarly article	3 points
I Internet site	1 point
Evaluation of the Internet site	2 points
Correct use of APA style	4 points
TOTAL	30 points

GEL Library Module
Fall 2002

Gabriela Sonntag, Library (ask for me at Circulation Desk as my office is not in a public area) Phone: (760) 750-4356 Email: gsg@csusm.edu

During this library module you will be gaining the skills needed to be successful in this class and in your future college career. We will focus on the college level research skills that will make your time spent researching productive! This module is organized using the *Information literacy competency standards for higher education.* Similar to other standards for higher education (such as accreditation standards or *Workforce 2000* standards) these standards (listed below FYI) outline exactly what you will need to know and be able to do in this module:

I. Standard One:
Develop a thesis statement; describe the role of general information sources to increase familiarity with a topic; identify key concepts and terms for their topic; recognize disciplinarity in organization of information; identify purpose and audience of resources (popular v. scholarly); use a variety of methods for acquiring information; develop a realistic research plan; develop and describe criteria used to make information decisions and choices.

II. Standard Two:
Investigate scope, content and organization of info systems; select approaches for accessing information; identify keywords, synonyms and related terms; select controlled vocabulary (LCSH, Thesaurus); construct search strategy (Booleans, etc.); implement search strategy; use various search systems (PAC and indexes); use classification schemes; use ILL and other document delivery services; assess the search results; differentiate between types of sources cited and understand elements of citation; record citation information; use various technologies.

III. Standard Three:
Reads text and selects main ideas; restates concepts in own terms; identifies verbatim material to quote; examines and compares information to evaluate; determines whether information satisfies search; uses criteria to determine if information contradicts or verifies other information used; draws conclusions; determines probable accuracy, selects information that provides evidence; participates in class discussions; determines if information need is met; reviews search strategy; reviews information sources used and expands as needed.

IV. Standard Four:
The research guide: Organizes content; manipulates digital text; maintains journal of process; reflects on process; incorporates principles of design; communicates clearly.

California State University, San Marcos

V. Standard Five:
Identifies and discusses issues of free vs. fee-based information (Internet); identifies and discusses issues of censorship and free speech; demonstrates understanding of intellectual property, copyright, etc.; complies with institutional policies on access to information; legally obtains, stores, and disseminates text, data, and images; demonstrates understanding of plagiarism; selects appropriate documentation style.

Grading for this module will be based on:
> Research Guide-- 50 points
> Home work-- 50 points
> In-class activities-- 50 points

Total for library module-- 150 points

> **Day One:** The objective of this first day is to learn Library of Congress classification system and subject headings, how they relate to each other and how to use them to find information effectively and efficiently! Activity: 1.0 points. Homework: *Research Guide: 50 points* due on last day of Library Module.

> **Day Two:** The objective of this day is to organize our research. During a visit to the Library you will learn more about the types of resources available and finding information on your topic of choice. Worksheet: 10 points. Homework: Thesis statement and report of the research plan 1.5 points

> **Day Three (lab): FOR DAY THREE YOU MUST HAVE YOUR EMAIL USER ID AND PASSWORD ACTIVATED** Using your research plan you will begin to find information using the online catalog. You will also learn about citation styles and begin using the APA style for citing your sources. Keyword versus subject searching will be emphasized. Worksheet: 1.0 points. Homework: Bibliography of at least two books on your topic in correct APA style. 10 points

> **Day Four (lab):** The objective of today is to learn about the various indexes and databases available for research. Booleans, search strategy as well as the difference between popular and scholarly sources will be emphasized. Worksheet: 1.0 points. Homework: You will write abstracts, annotations and evaluations of 2 sources found - a popular and a scholarly article on your topic. I5 points

> **Day Five (lab):** Today we will explore the good, bad and ugly of the Internet! Worksheet: 10 points. Homework: Annotated bibliography of 5 websites on your topic. 10 points

> **Day Six:** Putting it all together. Going from the sources found to the successful paper written!

Course Outline

Class Number	**Topic**
<u>1</u>	Course introduction, Introduction to Information, Pretest to determine computer skill level. Introduction to libraries and library materials.
<u>2</u>	What is information? How it is organized? Steps of the research process.
<u>3</u>	The Wizard OPAC, how to get the best information? Boolean logic and basic search strategies
<u>4</u>	Using CD-ROMS and microforms, Interlibrary Loan and other library services. Types of indices and abstracts
<u>5</u>	Introduction of Internet Explorer, Netscape, and the WWW. Introduction to WWW search engines, Critical evaluation of information sources
<u>6</u>	Library of Congress subject headings, Basic Keyword searching of online databases, Using the Internet
<u>7</u>	Quiz, review of answers
<u>8</u>	Full-text databases, ProQuest Direct, Wilson Web, secrets of effective searching
<u>9</u>	Specialized encyclopedias, Specialized indices – web-based and print sources. (PsychInfo, PsychArticles online)
<u>10</u>	Free your mind and think in synonyms
<u>11</u>	Copyright issues, Net-etiquette, Ethical and legal use of information.
<u>12</u>	Review of bibliography lists, Citation formats
<u>13</u>	Using a fee-based service
<u>14</u>	Checking for author background, bias, audience
<u>15</u>	Final exam, Bibliography due.

Developed by: Deborah West, Head Reference Librarian

Lynchburg College

GS113 eResearch in the College Library
Fall Semester 2002
Tuesdays & Thursdays 2:30 to 3:45 10/17/02- 12/05/02
Class meets in EIRC: Library Computer Lab

Instructor: Ms. E.F. Henderson
Office: Library 1st floor, Instructional Services Office (next to Popular Music CDs)
Office Hours: Mon. Tues. Thurs, and Fri. 9a.m. - 5 p.m., Wed. 3p.m. - 10p.m., 544-8442 - henderson@lynchburg.edu

The focus of this course will be on using online resources for college level research purposes. Assignments will cover advanced search strategies for online journal indexes and critical analysis of suitable topics, plus the difference between WEB subject directories and search engines and when and how to retrieve the best results for each type. How to evaluate WEB resources and cite them in a bibliography will be emphasized.

COURSE GOALS:

Upon successful completion of this course, students will be able to:

- o   Identify the types of Internet resources available that are useful for general academic applications;
- o   successfully use WEB and library catalogs, directories, indexes and other databases to find specific information resources via the Internet;
- o   clearly describe how information is arranged, accessed and made available via the Internet; critically evaluate the quality and usefulness of Internet information resources;
- o   develop search strategies on a specific topic, gather and evaluate Internet information on this topic and present a bibliography of the of the research and written evaluation of the search process; and access selected class materials and submit assignments electronically.

Attendance is required. Absences will be excused ONLY with prior notification or a note from the Dean of Students office after the fact. Sudden illnesses and family emergencies fall into the last category. At minimum you are expected to leave voicemail or e-mail prior to class time, if you are unable to attend class. All missed work must be made up. Each unexcused absence will result in the deduction of one point from the final grade.

RESERVE TEXT: *Searching Smart on the World Wide Web* **by Cheryl Gould**

Assignments will take the form of classroom group work and individual assignments. There will be an in-class exam and a final project consisting of a written guide to web resources on a topic of the student's choosing (approved by the instructor) and an oral presentation of a critical evaluation of one of the Web pages from the Bibliography. In addition an analysis and comparison of two of the periodical indexes available online through the Library Desktop will be a required project.

The periodical index project will be due November 12th. The web bibliography project will be due by 5:00 p.m., December 1 1th. Papers turned in after that time will automatically be lowered one letter grade. The

Worksheets and online assignments	80 pts: (40%)
Periodical Indexes anlaysis project	30 pts: (15%)
Written exam	30 pts: (15%)
Website analysis and presentation	40 pts: (20%)
Attendance and class participation	20 pts: (10%)
Total 200 pts (100%)	

final project will not be accepted after December 14th without a written excuse from the Dean of Students' Office.

Semester grades will be calculated as follows:

Grade calculations are based on percentages as follows:

A+	>97% (196-200pts)	C+	78%-79%(156-159pts)
A	93%-97% (186-195pts)	C	73%-77%(146-155pts)
A-	90%-92% (180-184pts)	C-	70%-72%(140-145pts)
B+	88%-89% (176-179pts)	D+	68%-69%(136-139pts)
B	83%-87% (166-175pts)	D	63%-67%(126-135pts)
B-	80%-82% (160-165pts)	D-	60%-62%(120-125pts)
		F	<60% (0-119pts)

Students will be expected to access and submit some of the worksheet assignments online through the Blackboard account. There will be a class email distribution list. I will use the list to communicate with the class so I recommend you check it on a regular basis. Instructions on accessing the online resources will be given in class at the appropriate time.

Schedule of topics for class rneeting
(subject to change if need arises)

10/17 TH	Introduction to types of online Resources	Scavenger Hunt Assignment #1;
10/22 T	Boolean Logic	Assignment #2 Read Gould, pg.26-27 & 41-44 "Advanced Search Features"
10/24 TH	Expanded Academic ASAP,	Assignment #3 Explore general dbs
10/29 T	ArticleFirst Lexis-Nexis, Dow Jones	Assignment #4
10/31 TH	WorldCat, CSA, IDEAL, & JSTOR	Assignment #5 Index comparison topic due
11/5 T	Metadata, Indexing, & evaluating Websites	Assignment #6 human vs. machine indexing. Gould pgs. 19-25 & 45-50
11/7 TH	Library Links Lists, Subject Directories	Assignment #7
11/12 T	Subject directories cont. **Index comparison due**	Assignment #8
11/14 TH	Go direct to the Source	Assignment #9, Gould pg.57-63
11/19 T	Search Engines	Assignment # 10, Gould 3 7-41 Review 4 1-44
11/21 TH	Search Engines	Assignment #11,
11/26 T	Search Engines	
11/28 TH	Ethics and the Internet, written exam	
12/2 T	Presentations	
12/5 TH	Presentations/Final Bibliography due	

Saint Francis University

CORE 101: Information Literacy

Topic Coverage   Fall / Spring 2002- 2003

Classes convene one-day per week for one hour over the 14 week term.   Half of our first-year students have Core 101 in the Fall; the remaining half during the Spring term.   Fall/Spring 2000/2001 instruction did not include Excel.

Laptop Use/ Windows Environment	Microsoft Word
Creating files and folders	Page Layout and editing commands
Formatting a disk	Setting margins, tabs
Saving to student F:\ drivespace	Using find and replace commands
Copying/Cutting/Pasting	Page numbering, footnotes
Working with multiple applications	Inserting symbols
	Using tables
	Saving and backing-up files
	Inserting graphics
Groupwise Mail program	**Microsoft Excel**
Mail folders; Set up "Copies to Self" and others.	Excel overview
	Spreadsheets and Excel worksheets
Signature Block	Basic data manipulation
Distribution Lists	Worksheet layout
Save to Disk	Copying cell contents
Attaching files to email	

Database Use	Microsoft PowerPoint
FRANCIS	Overview of PowerPoint
PALCI	Editing text in slides
FirstSearch	Using various views
Proquest	Inserting clip-art, graphics and tables
Netfirst	Controlling presentation effects
JSTOR	Adding speaker's notes
Additional resources as appropriate	Printing options
Off-campus access to databases	
Research Topics	**Webpage Development**
Ethics in research	Use of Microsoft Frontpage
Plagiarism	Basic webpage creation
Style-guides; Use of the Holt Handbook	Using backgrounds and text variations
Works-cited page format	Inserting images, links and tables
Evaluating quality of sources	Additional insert features of Frontpage 2000
Research and computer-related terminology	Evaluation of website content
Internet and WWW	**WebCT Environment**
Search Engines	Class content is presented using WebCT courseware to familiarize students with this environment.
Hyperlinks and URL's	
Effective search strategies and resources	
Criteria to evaluate information quality	

CORE 101 Information Literacy
ST. Francis University

Instructor:

<u>Brian Anater, MLS</u>

Rationale: This course deals with the basics of effective research and the use of technology to manage it. You will learn to distinguish and use various resources available at the Pasquerilla Library which will aid you in beginning your research efforts. You will also improve your strategy of selecting from among the numerous information resources currently available online and in print and learn effective technologies to utilize them.

Objectives:
1) to acquire a practical knowledge of the resources, especially online resources, of an academic library;
2) to formulate appropriate strategies and technological understanding to satisfy informational needs;
3) to become familiar with the purpose, use and arrangement of a core group of basic reference works
4) to develop an awareness of and an appreciation for scholarship and the resources by which it is conveyed and shared in a library setting.

Policies & Procedures:
Attendance: Strongly recommended; Class attendance earns one point to a maximum of 15 points toward class grade. Work will be completed, to a large degree, in class. If you are unable to attend class for an excusable reason, you should contact your instructor. Be sure to sign the attendance sheet when entering class every week.

Required Work: Attendance in class; completion of weekly assignments which should be handed in at the beginning of the following class each week; as well as completion of a mid-term and a final exam.

All assignments must be completed by the last week of class to count toward course credit. Incomplete assignments are subject to partial scoring.

Credits: One credit per 15 week session .

NOTICE: A grade of 60% or higher in Information Literacy is necessary to pass Core 101.

Grading Scale : Plus/Minus grading will be used, within the grade categories as follows:

below 60 = F, 60 - 69.99 = D, 70 - 78.99 = C, 79 = C+, 80 = B-, 81-88.9 = B, 89= B+, 90= A-, 91-100=A

The following table illustrates the proportional weight of class activities:

Class participation	15%
Reference Questions	20%
Assigned Worksheets	30%
Exams	29%
Works-Cited Paper	10%
TOTAL	100%

Available at: http://www.francis.edu/newsfc/library/ref/coretopics.htm

Library Research 102 **Spring (Term I) 2003**	**Instructors:** Ramsey Library Faculty **Phone:** 251-6111 (Reference Desk)

Library Research 102, a one-credit course, provides an introduction to library resources and research tools. Students are expected to read assigned Web modules, gain hands-on experience using library resources in a laboratory setting through completion of in-class exercises, and consult with reference librarians whenever they have questions.

Objectives

After completing Library Research 102, students should be able to:

- approach a research assignment with a logical strategy.
- select appropriate print and online sources for specific research needs.
- use the library's electronic resources effectively (including the online library catalog and periodical indexes).
- locate resources in Ramsey Library such as books, journals, media and government documents.
- make use of the various services offered by Ramsey Library.
- approach research and information retrieval with enhanced critical thinking skills.

Class Policies

Attendance

You are required to attend: **(a) the first class session** for a general introduction to the course and a tour of the library; **(b) three lab sessions** with your instructor in the library to gain hands-on experience using some key electronic resources for research; and **(c) the final exam** must also be passed to successfully complete this course.

Withdrawals/Incompletes

Wednesday, Feb. 5, 2003 is the last day to withdraw from the class with a grade of "W." See the UNCA Catalog for the statement of regulations governing withdrawals and incompletes.

Required Lab Exercise Sessions

You are required to put some of the material covered in assigned readings into practice in three hands-on lab sessions in the library. This means that **you must attend all lab class sessions with your instructor at the regularly scheduled class time for your assigned group / day**. If you miss one or more labs, you will not be eligible to take the final exam.

Final Exam

The final exam covers information both from the assigned readings, and from the in-class lab exercises. It consists of thirty (30) multiple-choice, matching, true-false and fill-in-the-blank questions, and takes approximately 30-40 minutes to complete.

The exam for your section of LR 102 will be administered during the fifth and final class session.

Participation

Participating is defined as taking part, as having a part or sharing in something. **It is expected and required for you to be an active member of the class.** Participation encompasses taking part in class discussions, working on and completing in-class exercises and contributing to an overall learning atmosphere. Signs that indicate you are **not** a fully participating class member include checking email, surfing the web unrelated to assignments and even napping during class exercises, discussions or presentations. (Note: some instructors may also give pop quizzes.)

Grading

Grading is S/U (Satisfactory or Unsatisfactory). This grade is based on your satisfactory participation and completion of the three required lab exercises and your score on the final exam. **A passing grade for the course is 84% or higher – no exceptions.** If you fail to complete all required labs or do not pass the exam, you will receive a "U" and must repeat the course in another semester. The grade breakdown is as follows:

Lab 1	20%
Lab 2	20%
Lab 3	20%
Final Exam	40%

Students with Disabilities

Students with disabilities should contact the Office of Liberal Arts Learning and Disability Services (251-6980) in order to arrange for alternate accommodations in this course.

Required Reading Modules:

These assigned readings are available on the Web, and are required reading prior to completing each lab exercise. You can also access them by clicking on the Library Research Course page.

Lab 1 -- Intro to Research / Using the Library Catalog

- Overview of Ramsey Services and Departments
- Locations and Call Numbers
- Subject Searches and Keyword Searches
- Using Boolean Operators

Lab 2 -- Using a Periodical Index / Finding Articles

- Reference Tools You Should Know About
- Developing a Library Research Strategy
- Scholarly Journals vs. Magazines

- Finding Information in Periodicals

Lab 3 -- Finding and Evaluating Web Information

- Analyzing Information Sources
- Using the Web for Research
- Evaluating Web Information

Recommended (Optional) Reading:

Making Sense of Library Research: A Guide for Undergraduate Students (University of North Carolina at Asheville, 2001 Revised Edition).

- This useful text is available on the Web. You can access it by clicking Library Research Course from the Ramsey Library home page, or by pointing your browser directly to: http://bullpup.lib.unca.edu/library/lr/txtbk/txtbk.html

---

Last updated 9 December 2002.

Keys to Success in LR 102

▶ Take the Required Labs, Seriously

Not only is successfully completing the lab assignments good for you, they will aid you in answering specific questions on the final exam. The labs are a course requirement, so take them seriously and please be on time.

▶ Get Started! Don't Procrastinate!

LR 102 is a brief Term 1 course, so don't wait until the fourth week to begin studying for the final exam! This is a practical class that may help you right away in your other courses, so be kind to yourself. Complete the labs as scheduled and study up early in the semester.

▶ Study the Readings

Each assigned reading contains basic concepts of library research and specific information about Ramsey Library resources and services. Studying the readings is important for passing the exam. Even if you are a frequent library user or have done library research, you still need to complete the assigned readings.

▶ Attend All Required Lab Sessions

Check your syllabus for your lab group class / day meeting dates. And remember, all three lab session exercises must be completed before taking the final in-class exam.

▶ Ask for Help

When in doubt, ask! It is our hope that you will see Ramsey Library as an open and friendly place where you can always ask questions. Reference librarians and LR 102 instructors are always happy to help.

Last updated 31 July 2002.

Available at: http://bullpup.lib.unca.edu/Library/lr/102sylspr03.html

000770

Page design & original content Copyright 2002 by Jim Alderman.

LIS1001
Beginning Library and Information Systems Strategies (BLISS)

Course Description: LIS1001 is designed to acquaint the novice researcher with both traditional and computerized means of classifying, storing, and retrieving information, and will focus on the library as an information storage and retrieval center. LIS1001 emphasizes critical thinking and research skills and is especially recommended to freshmen.

Course Goals: LIS1001 is designed to develop student competencies in the use of both traditional (printed) and computerized library and information resources. LIS1001 will provide students with a working knowledge of types of information resources available and how these resources enable efficient location of information in a university library. Skills developed in the course will transfer to any academic setting and will lay the groundwork for successful completion of research methods courses within the various academic disciplines. Upon completion of LIS1001, students will be able to:

- Find appropriate reference sources and indexes for identifying research materials
- Efficiently use indexes and library catalogues, both printed and computerized
- Understand the organization of a university library
- Locate materials in any collection of a university library
- Plan and organize a research project
- Select and adequately narrow a research topic
- Use critical thinking skills in evaluating sources
- Demonstrate a facility for doing research and using libraries

Transferrable Skills: LIS1001 will prepare students for better performance in a number of other core courses now offered at the university. In that the course develops research techniques, it will better prepare students for junior level research methods courses currently offered. LIS1001 will also complement research skills developed in ENC1102 and, if taken before ENC1102, should enable better performance in completing research projects required in that course.

Key Concepts Covered in LIS1001

- Systems of Classification and the need for such systems (Library of Congress, Superintendent of Documents, Dewey Decimal)
- Guides to Classification Systems (print and online thesauri, subject headings, descriptors, key words, etc.)
- Types of Materials to be used in completing research (monographs, serials, indices, abstracting services, electronic/online services, primary/secondary sources, reference works, microformat services, etc.)
- Bibliographic Styles (MLA, APA, Turabian, Chicago, etc.)
- Bibliographies/Annotated Bibliographies
- Plagiarism (What it is and how to avoid it)
- The Internet and the World Wide Web
- Research Process (Its importance to intellectual growth; how to choose and narrow topics; how to select and evaluate material in support of a topic)
- Information Retrieval Systems (print, online, cd-rom)

Enabling Activities

- **Classification of Knowledge:** Students will examine various formal classification systems and learn how they are used to organize materials into subject areas. Print and online uses of the systems will be demonstrated. To reinforce the usefulness of classification, students will be given exercises that can be completed with or without knowledge of classification. Results will demonstrate that knowledge of the system produces better and more complete results.
- **Types of Research Materials:** Students will be shown different types of materials that can be used in completing research (books, magazines, journals, bibliographies, encyclopedias, conference proceedings, etc.) and will be given explanations of what each type of source can offer. Written assignments will demonstrate the student's recognition of the differences between the various materials. Emphasis will be placed on judicious selection of materials based on the research need, that is, when to use magazine or newspaper articles and when to use journals or conference proceedings.
- **Bibliographies/Annotated Bibliographies:** Students may select individual topics to

research and will compile both non-annotated and annotated bibliographies covering the topics. Correct bibliographic form will be stressed. Attention will be given to the accepted style of presentation for various disciplines (MLA, APA, etc.).

- **Electronic and Microformat Materials:** Students will use a number of non-print sources to locate and retrieve materials in support of a research topic. Students will learn the difference between abstracting services and full text services and be familiar with using microformat materials.

- **Internet and World Wide Web:** Students will explore the Internet and retrieve representative documents from the Web. Students will learn to use various search engines, such as AltaVista, Lycos, and HotBot to find relevant materials on the Internet. Critical in this exploration is student understanding of how to distinguish between factual materials and opinion or mere gossip.

- **Plagiarism:** This concept will be developed through lecture and in-class discussion of what constitutes plagiarism. When given printed examples of original sources and their secondary citings, students will be able to determine which are plagiarized and which are not. Students will also learn the academic and legal consequences of plagiarism.

- **The Research Process:** Students will discuss the importance of the research process to academic achievement and the further growth of knowledge. Students will be asked to research a topic that demonstrates the importance of research to the world community and to deliver a brief presentation on how they discovered their topics and the current access points for learning more about the topic.

The goal of all activities and exercises is to give students hands-on experience with as many research tools as possible. A strong emphasis will be placed on emerging technologies and the developing Information Superhighway. Once students have completed the course, they should feel comfortable in any research environment and be able to quickly choose the appropriate tools for locating materials necessary to successful completion of their projects.

005102

Page design &
original content
Copyright 2002
by Jim Alderman.

What is BLISS?

BLISS IS NOT IGNORANCE! A good dictionary definition of **bliss** is **complete happiness**. Although we can't guarantee students complete happiness upon successful completion of LIS1001, we can guarantee that completing research projects will be much easier.

Research can be stressful for people who are unfamiliar with libraries and research systems. BLISS helps researchers develop familiarity with libraries and research systems and thus helps to eliminate much of the stress usually associated with college courses. Of course, knowing how to do research doesn't necessarily guarantee success in a college course. A successful student must have good writing skills, motivation, and the desire to succeed. Having good research skills can help, though, by saving a student time, time that can be used for reading course materials, for polishing written assignments, and for assimilating ideas.

BLISS shows students how to locate information fast in libraries, in online databases, and on the Internet. Anyone can find information. But finding the best information available can often be time-consuming and tricky. LIS1001 will help students to become efficient researchers, researchers able to quickly sift through mountains of information and find the best information on any topic.

Does BLISS sound like your key to becoming a good academic researcher? It is. Join us for a semester of learning how to find information fast and discover bliss for yourself.

001260

Page design & original content Copyright 2002 by Jim Alderman.

LIS1001 -- BEGINNING LIBRARY AND INFORMATION SYSTEMS STRATEGIES

SYLLABUS

Instructors:

Mary Davis, Coordinator of Bibliographic Instruction
Jim Alderman, Associate University Librarian

Section 37 Meeting Time: Monday, 12:00 to 12:50 PM.
Section 38 Meeting Time: Wednesday, 12:00 to 12:50 PM.

Location: Building 12, Room 4005

Office Hours: By Arrangement

Text: Readings online.

Prerequisites: None

Corequisites: Although there are no corequisites for LIS1001, students may find the course more useful if taken at the same time as a course requiring substantial research, such as English Composition or research methods courses within a student's degree program.

Course Objectives:

Upon completion of LIS1001 students will:

- understand how knowledge is organized in library collections;
- be familiar with and understand the uses of major research tools necessary for successful completion of academic coursework (indexes, bibliographies, online services, Internet resources);
- be able to do research in a university library using both traditional printed sources and computerized resources with minimal assistance from library staff; and
- be able to choose and analyze the appropriateness of resources chosen on a given topic.

Course Requirements and Class Attendance: Class attendance is required. Even one missed class can jeopardize successful completion of the course. Students will be responsible for timely completion of reading assignments and written assignments and will be required to participate in class discussions and any group or individual presentations assigned during the semester.

Written Assignments: Assignments will include periodic quizzes (announced in advance), exercises that reinforce learning, and discussion group postings in the course Blackboard site.

Grading: The final grade for the class will be based on completion of the following criteria:

Assignments/Exercises	40%
Quizzes	40%
Class Participation/Attendance	10%
Discussion Group Postings	10%

Instructional Goals: Our primary goal for the class is for LIS1001 students to be skilled and self-reliant information seekers by semester's end.

Available at: http://www.unf.edu/~alderman/BLISS2/index.html

Library Science 101

Library Science 101A: Library Resources in the Humanities

Course Syllabus

Syllabus Index

- Instructor Information
- Course Information
- Objectives
- Requirements
- Class Attendance
- Assignments
- Grading
- Readings
- Policies and Special Considerations
- Other Information
- Useful Links
- Course Schedule

Instructor Information

Instructor: Heidi Lowry
Email: hlowry@sewanee.edu
Phone: 598-1709
Office: Room 141, Main Floor, duPont Library
Office Hours: Drop in or by appointment
Reference email: askref@sewanee.edu
Reference phone: 598-1368
Class Time: Tuesdays, 2:00 P.M.
Classroom: ATC Mac Classroom (Ground Floor, duPont Library)

Course Information

From the course catalog:

This course introduces students to the organization, collections and services of an academic library and enables them to become more competent in finding, evaluating and using electronic and traditional print resources in the humanities. The Internet, CD-ROMs, and various electronic databases are included. (Pass/Fail Only, half course) Please note that you can only receive credit for LS101 *once*.

University of the South

From the instructor:

This course introduces students to research methods and resources that will make the search for information a more effective, efficient process. The methods learned here can be directly applied to present and future research for both scholarly and personal information needs. To achieve these goals, the classes will involve some lecture, group work and discussion, and activities both in and out of class to gain hands-on experience with research sources and techniques.

Course Objectives

At the end of this course, you will know:

- How to define and focus a topic for a research paper
- What resources are available for research in and through the library
- How to select the best resources to use
- How to use the resources you find
- How to evaluate the resources and the information you find

Course Requirements

1. Be in class each week (see the attendance guidelines below and in the Student Handbook); every time we meet brings you the chance to learn about something new that will help you.
2. Share your thoughts, ideas, ask and answer questions, and otherwise contribute to the class activities; what you share will help someone, including your instructor.
3. Complete your activities and assignments on time in a professional manner; each one relates to the others and reflects upon you as well.

Class Attendance

Students are expected to attend all classes. The only valid reasons for missing class are illness or family bereavement. If you are going to be absent for any of these reasons, please try and let me know before the class. Any student missing two classes for unexplained reasons will be put on cut warning.

If you have missed a class for a valid reason, I will gladly help you catch up when you return. If you've missed a class for any other reason, you will have to depend upon the generosity of your fellow students to catch up with your class notes. In either situation, you will need to make up the assignment which you can get from me.

Assignments

In-class exercises:

- You will often have exercises to do during class that give you practice with research methods and resources that we discuss in class.
- These exercises are due during class and count towards your participation grade.

Take-home assignments:

- You will have take-home assignments that give you practice with research methods and resources that we discuss in class.
- These take-home assignments are due on the Friday after they are assigned (see details in the Grading section of this syllabus).
- You will be expected to make-up any assignments that you miss.
- At the beginning of the term, you have 4 "lifelines" which can be used if you cannot pass in an assignment on time. For example, if you pass in an assignment 2 days late, you have used up 2 lifelines. Once you use your 4 lifelines, every other remaining assignment must be passed in on time--no exceptions! An assignment turned in on the Monday before class will use up 1 lifeline. An assignment turned in on Tuesday (a week after it was assigned) will use up 2 lifelines.
- Please let me know of any corrections or improvements you have for the assignments.
- Your final assignment will be an annotated bibliography or pathfinder of useful information sources for a specific topic.

Grading

- Take-home assignments are assigned on Tuesday at the end of class. They are due the following Friday by 5:00 PM.
- You will obtain a 'P' and pass this class when you fulfill the requirements listed in this syllabus and attain at least 700 out of a possible 1000 possible points from:
    - 250| Homework assignments
    - 150| In-class exercises
    - 350| Final project
    - 250| Attendance & class participation

University of the South

Course Readings

There will be readings that we will discuss in class, specific details on those to be announced. Also, there are books in the reference collection and on reserve with information that will better prepare you for the ideas and methods presented in class. Below is a select list of those books:

Reserve Material

Blazek, Ron and Elizabeth Aversa. *The Humanities: A Selective Guide to Information Sources..* 5th ed. Colorado: Libraries Unlimited, 2000. (General Collection AZ 221.B53 2000)

Gates, Jean Key. *Guide to the Use of Libraries and Information Sources.* 7th ed. New York: McGraw, 1994. (Reference Collection Z 710.G27 1994 - 1 hour reserve)

Gibaldi, Joseph. *MLA Handbook for Writers of Research Papers.* 5th ed. New York: MLA, 1999. (LB2369 .G53 1999 - 1 hour reserve; Several copies available in Reference)

Mann, Thomas. *The Oxford Guide to Library Research.* New York: Oxford UP, 1998. (Z 710.M23 1998 - 3 hour reserve)

Policies and Special Considerations

The Honor Code will be upheld in this as in any other course. While in-class activities and discussions will at times require that you share ideas and work with other students, you will not continue that in homework assignments and the final project done outside of class.

This class will be held in the Library building; please adhere to library policies. This class will also be held in a computer classroom; please use the computers only during computer-based in-class activities. Do not use the computers during lectures or presentations.

Please speak with me as soon as possible if you feel you may need assistance or accommodations due to a disability.

Other Information

Please feel free to talk to me about any questions you may have regarding this syllabus or this course. The information in this syllabus is subject to change.

Course Schedule

Class and Description	Dates	Assignment Due
Class 1 - Introduction to LS101, each other, and Library Tour	Tuesday, January 15th <u>Your Research Process assignment</u>	Friday, January 18th at 5:00
Class 2 - Catch-up Introductions, and the Research Process	January 22nd	Wednesday, January 30th at 9:00 a.m.
Class 3 - No Class -- Instructor out of town	January 29th	
Class 4 - the Research Process and Beyond	February 5th	Friday, February 8th at 5:00
Class 5 - Electronic Index Exploration	February 12th	
Class 6 - More Electronic Index Exploration	February 19th <u>Questia assignment</u>	Friday, February 22nd by 5:00
Class 7 - Test	February 26th	
Class 8 - Review and talk about <u>Final Project</u>	March 5th <u>Annotated Bibliography Assignment</u>	Monday, March 11th by Noon
Class 9 - No class	March 12th	
Spring Break	March 13th through 24th	
Class 10 - Electronic Journals	March 26th <u>Electronic Journal Assignment</u>	Monday, April 1st
Class 11 - Information on the Internet a.k.a. the Web	April 2nd <u>Web Searching and Website Assignment</u>	Monday, April 8th
Class 12 - Evaluating Information on the Web	April 9th <u>Career Search Information</u>	Monday, April 15th
Class 13 - Government Information	April 16th <u>Find Government Information</u>	Monday, April 22nd
Class 14 - Annotated Bibliography	April 23rd <u>Sample Bibliography</u>	Friday, May 3rd by 5:00 p.m.

Available at: http://ls101.sewanee.edu/A/info/syllabus.html

Wayne State College

GST 196-22: Basic Research Skills
August 27 - October 17, 2002
TR 2:00 - 2:50pm

Instructor: Gayle A. Poirier Documents/Reference Librarian Meet in Conn Library, Room 18 or as noted below. e-mail: gapoiri1@wsc.edu	Office: Room 28, Conn Library Lower Level Phone: 402-375-7419 1-800-228-9972 fax: 402-375-7538 Home Page: http://academic.wsc.edu/conn_library/contacts/staff/gayle/

Welcome to our course!! Basic Research Skills is an introductory course in learning to use library and Internet resources for research. It develops skills in searching online catalogs, Internet search engines, full-text databases and printed sources, including government documents and statistics. There are no tests or exams. A textbook is required for exercises and readings. Much of your work will be in the form of hands-on Web exercises, class discussions, and activities. The final project offers an opportunity to use what you've learned in a meaningful way.

Course Objectives:
By the end of this course, you will be able to:

- use basic search techniques in tools such as CONNection (the library's online catalog) to retrieve books, reference works, government documents and statistics; printed indexes and online databases such as *EbscoHost* to find magazine and journal articles; and the Internet for a variety of information;
- critically select and evaluate the resources you find;
- distinguish between popular and scholarly works, and between primary and secondary sources;
- design and implement an effective library search strategy. This will include selecting an appropriate topic, then accessing, selecting, evaluating, retrieving, and documenting a variety of sources on the topic. There is no research paper requirement.

Required Text:
Bolner, Myrtle S. and Gayle A. Poirier. *The Research Process: Books and Beyond.* Dubuque, IA: Kendall/Hunt Publishing Company, 2002. (2nd ed., Revised printing.) The text is used for readings, assignments, class activities, etc. Purchase only a new copy of the text; exercise pages are removed for assignments. Copies should be available in both campus bookstores.

Attendance
Because of the nature of this course, it is imperative that you attend <u>each</u> session and participate in the activities of the class.
If you are unable to attend for any reason, please notify me to make arrangements to make up the material.

Grading and Course Requirements:
Course grades will be submitted on December 20, 2002. Assignments are graded on a 400 point scale:

A = 360 - 400   B= 320 - 359   C - 280 - 319   D= 240 - 279   F= 239 and below
No late assignments without prior approval.

Course Requirements:

MTG	DATE	PLACE	CONTENT	ASSIGN	DUE	POINTS	READINGS
1	8/27 TU	Rm 18	Introduction: Getting to Know Resources	- - -	- -	- - -	Ch.3
2	8/29 TH	Rm 18	Questioning Sources	1: Eval. Mats	9/3	25/ extra 5/	Ch.4 & 5
3	9/3 TU	Rm 18	Where Do I Start?	- - -	- -	- - -	Ch.1 &.7
4	9/5 TH	Lab 210	Benefits of Organized Searching	2: Elec.Search	9/10	40/	- - -
5	9/10 TU	Ref Rm	Tips for Fast Finds	- - -	- -	- - -	Ch.11&12
6	9/12 TH	Rm 18	Did You Know...? People and Their Work	3: Ref. Mats	9/17	55/	- - -
7	9/17 TU	Rm 18	Discussion & Review	Chap. Review Q	- -	extra 5/	Ch.8
8	9/19 TR	Ref Rm	Finding Those Articles!	4: Periodicals	9/26	60/	- - -
9	9/24 TU	Lab 210	Databases & E-Journals	- - -	- -	- - -	Ch.6
10	9/26 TH	Lab 210	What About the 'Net?: Engines,	**5: Internet**	10/1	60/	Ch.9

			Directories and more				
11	10/1 TU	Gov Docs	Uncle Sam's Works	- - -	- -		Ch.10
12	10/3 TH	Lab 210	Using Numbers	6: Gov & Stats	10/8	60/	Ch.2
13	10/8 TU	Rm 18	Understanding Research	Topic	10/10	15/	
14	10/10 TH	Rm 18	Review Project Instructions; Approve Topic/Thesis/Outline	Projects	- -	85/	- - -
15	10/15 TU	Rm 18	Oral Project Presentations	- - -	- -	- - -	- - -
16	10/17 TH	Rm 18	Oral Presentations: All Typed Final Projects Due	- - -	- -	- - -	- - -

TOTAL POINTS POSSIBLE: 400

A = 360 - 400   B= 320 - 359   C - 280 - 319   D= 240 - 279   F= 239 and below
No late assignments accepted without prior approval.

Grades will be posted by 5 p.m., December 23, 2002. You may view your work in my office at any time with an appointment. Good luck with your work and have a great semester!
9/24/02 revised

Available at: http://academic.wsc.edu/faculty/gapoiri1/basic_skills/syllabus.html

IFL 101
Requirements and Policies for All Sections

Information Literacy

The goal of this course is to assist students in developing skills which will enable them to function as information literate individuals capable of using and applying current information technology. Students in this course will learn to determine when information is required, and will develop skills in acquiring information using library resources and computer technologies. Students will learn effective searching, evaluation of information, and use of the World Wide Web and Internet.

--Taken from the York College of Pennsylvania *General Catalog 1997 - 1999*

Course Objectives

The students will be able to:

1. use information ethically
2. recognize that accurate and complete information is the basis for intelligent decision making
3. recognize when information is needed
4. develop successful search strategies based on an understanding of how information is organized
5. identify potential sources of information
6. evaluate information
7. use and communicate information effectively
8. use information in critical thinking and problem solving
9. select and apply appropriate technologies when accessing, obtaining, and organizing information for use
10. access the Internet, electronic mail and other forms of electronic communication
11. use word processors to create professional documents to convey information
12. use software to make professional presentations

Goals/Skills/Outcomes listed by course topic.

Academic Dishonesty

In cases where faculty members observe academic dishonesty, the student(s) so concerned will receive a grade of "F" or "0" for the course and a written report of this incident will be forwarded to the Academic Dean, through the appropriate department chairperson, for inclusion in a special file to be kept in the Dean's Office. Faculty members will send the student a copy of this report along with a statement of the consequences of such behavior. In cases where a student receives a second dishonesty report, the student will, under normal circumstances, be suspended from the college for one semester by the Academic Dean. The student may appeal through the normal appeals procedure. The Dean shall inform the Academic Standards Committee of the number of dishonesty reports submitted each semester and the disposition of any second dishonesty reports as they occur.

Course Requirements

- Attendance
- Class participation
- Written assignments
- Presentations
- Quizzes
- Group assignments

Methods will vary, but may include:
Class Workshops
Hands-on instruction
In-class assignments
Out-of-class work and assignments
Online demonstrations
Readings
Online exercises
Small group discussions
Small group presentations with demonstrations
Lecture
Quizzes
Final project

Grading

4	(A)	90-100 %
3	(B)	80-89 %
2	(C)	70-79%
1	(D)	60-69 %
0	(F)	below 60 %
I	incomplete work	

Research Strategies

All students should be able to

- recognize that accurate and complete information is the basis for intelligent decision making
- develop successful search strategies based on an understanding of how information is organized
- identify potential sources of information
- use information in critical thinking and problem solving

- **Skills**
  - Recognize how information is organized
  - Create search strategies
  - Use controlled vocabulary, keyword and natural language searches
- **Outcomes**
  - Understand how information is organized
  - Demonstrate search strategies
  - Decide what material is appropriate for assignments
  - Determine how to use unfamiliar search tools

Reference

All students should be able to

- recognize that accurate and complete information is the basis of intelligent decision making
- develop successful search strategies based on an understanding of how information is organized
- identify potential sources of information
- evaluate information
- use information in critical thinking and problem solving

- **Skills**
  - Use reference resources
- **Outcomes**
  - Understand the types of information available in reference resources

Books and AV

All students should be able to

- develop successful search strategies based on an understanding of how information is organized
- identify potential sources of information
- select and apply appropriate technologies when accessing, obtaining, and organizing information for use

- identify potential sources of information outside Schmidt Library

- **Skills**
  - o Formulate search strategies, execute searches, and interpret results
  - o Use Schmidt Library Catalog
  - o Use the ACLCP Online Catalog and other online catalogs
- **Outcomes**
  - o Understand the online catalog
  - o Know how to find local and worldwide resources

Periodicals

All students should be able to

- develop successful search strategies based on an understanding of how information is organized
- identify potential sources of information
- evaluate information
- use information in critical thinking and problem solving
- identify potential sources of information outside Schmidt Library

- **Skills**
  - o Use periodical indexes
  - o Determine Schmidt Library holdings
  - o Determine holdings in ACLCP and other libraries
  - o Find periodical articles
- **Outcomes**
  - o Understand how to use indexes to find periodical articles
  - o Know how to find local and worldwide resources

Internet

All students should be able to

- develop successful search strategies based on an understanding of how information is organized
- select and apply appropriate technologies when accessing, obtaining, and organizing information for use
- access the Internet, electronic mail and other forms of electronic communication
- evaluate information
- use information in critical thinking and problem solving

- **Skills**
  - o Use browsers
  - o Select and use search tools
  - o Access licensed library databases
  - o Differentiate types of World Wide Web sources

- **Outcomes**
  - Understand the strengths and weaknesses of the Internet
  - Identify credible Internet resources
  - Determine how to use unfamiliar search tools

Evaluation

All students should be able to

- recognize that accurate and complete information is the basis for intelligent decision making
- use information in critical thinking and problem solving

- **Skills**
  - Evaluate sources using specific criteria
- **Outcomes**
  - Critically evaluate all resources

Scholarly/Popular/Trade

All students should be able to

- recognize that accurate and complete information is the basis for intelligent decision making
- identify potential sources of information
- use information in critical thinking and problem solving

- **Skills**
  - Use popular, trade/professional and scholarly sources
- **Outcomes**
  - Understand how information is organized
  - Decide what material is appropriate for assignments

Primary/Secondary

All students should be able to

- recognize that accurate and complete information is the basis for intelligent decision making
- identify potential sources of information
- use information in critical thinking and problem solving

- **Skills**
  - Use primary and secondary sources
- **Outcomes**
  - Understand how information is organized
  - Decide what material is appropriate for assignments

York College of Pennsylvania

Ethics

All students should be familiar with

- YCP network policy
- YCP Student Handbook
- Copyright
- Plagiarism
- Ethical behavior in group work
- Consequences of unethical behavior

- **Skills**
  - Ability to make mature, informed judgments
- **Outcomes**
  - Use information ethically

Network Basics

All students should be able to

- select and apply appropriate technologies when accessing, obtaining, and organizing information for use
- access the Internet, electronic mail and other forms of electronic communication
- be familiar with network policy

- **Skills**
  - Log on and off the network
  - Save files to a personal home drive
  - Access additional programs including anti-virus software
  - Use basic Windows functions
- **Outcomes**
  - Effectively use the campus network to access programs and save files
  - Understand basic Windows concepts

Email/Newsgroups

All students should be able to

- use and communicate information effectively
- access the Internet, electronic mail and other forms of electronic communication
- use netiquette

- **Skills**
  - Use basic email functions
  - Apply netiquette
- **Outcomes**
  - Effectively communicate electronically

Visual Aids

All students should be able to

- use and communicate information effectively
- use presentation software to make professional presentations

- **Skills**
  - Use basic PowerPoint features
  - Create good graphic presentations
- **Outcomes**
  - Create an effective slide presentation
  - Understand basic graphics principles
  - Enhance oral and written presentations with good graphics

Documents

All students should be able to

- use and communicate information effectively
- use word processors to create professional documents to convey information

- **Skills**
  - Use basic Word features
  - Create good graphic presentations
- **Outcomes**
  - Apply basic Word features to create professional documents
  - Understand basic graphics principles
  - Enhance written presentations with good graphics

Evaluation

Evaluation Strategies
(All Types of Sources)

1. Evaluating Information: a Basic Checklist -- American Library Association flyer
2. How to Critically Analyze Information Sources -- Cornell University Library

Evaluation Strategies
(Internet & Web Sources)

1. Evaluating Internet Resources -- Laura Cohen and Trudi Jacobson / University of Albany Libraries
2. The Good, The Bad and the Ugly: or, Why It's a Good Idea to Evaluate Web Sources -- Susan Beck / New Mexico State University
3. Evaluating Web Resources -- Jan Alexander and Marsha Ann Tate / Widener University
4. Evaluating Internet Research Sources -- Robert Harris / Virtual Salt

---

Reserve Reading at Circulation Services:

1. Himmelfarb, Gertrude. "Revolution in the Library." *American Scholar* Spring 1997:197-204.
2. Fenton, Serena, et al. "Information Quality Checklist." *Technology and Learning* September 1998, 30.

Collection of Sites to Evaluate

1. Collection at York College of Pennsylvania
2. Collection at Widener University
3. Collection at New Mexico State: "The Good, the Bad, and the Ugly

Available at: http://www.ycp.edu/library/ifl/

Documents:
Tutorials

TO FIND BOOKS in Julia Rogers Library
SEARCH **OLLI**

Do a subject search:	Do a keyword search:
sports (Look at related headings and subheadings) women athletes coaches	women and sport* and (college* or universit*) coach* and soccer sport* and injur*

What's the difference between a SUBJECT and a KEYWORD search?

In a SUBJECT search, OLLI looks for the words you type only in the **subject** terms that are assigned to a book by the Library of Congress. The advantage of a subject search is that the books will definitely be about that subject. However, since these subject terms are not always consistently assigned, you may miss some good titles.

In a KEYWORD search, OLLI looks for the words you type in **subject, title, author, and contents** terms that are assigned to a book. The advantage of a keyword search is its comprehensiveness. However, since OLLI is finding terms in different places, you may get some irrelevant titles.

For best results, it's often a good idea to do both subject and keyword searches for your topic.

To find books in other libraries: Check Other Library Catalogs

---

Constructing a search strategy

What you must do - before you get online - to ensure a successful search :

- Know how to describe your research question (topic) in a sentence or phrase:

I want to find out why male enrollment in college is on the decline.

- dentify the concepts in your research question:

male   enrollment   college   decline

Goucher College

- Think of keywords which adequately describe your concepts:

male	enrollment	college	decline
men	attendance	universities	decrease

- Know how to connect your keywords:

(male* or men) and (enrol* or attend*) and (college* or universit*)
(male* or men) and (college* or universit*) and (declin* or decreas*)

More Search Tips

- Use wildcards for plurals and word variants when appropriate.

male* will find   male, males, malevolent, malefactor, etc.
   Use parentheses to enclose OR keywords.
(male* or men) and (enrol* or attend*) and (college* or universit*) and (declin* or decreas*)

Finding Journal Articles

What's in an electronic journal database?

citations:
The information you need to find the actual article:
author, title, source, date, page, volume.

abstracts:
Summaries of the articles

full text:
The text of the article is online.

General databases:
AcademicSearch Elite: Ebsco
An index with general coverage of the social sciences, humanities, sciences, and current events. With selected full-text.

WilsonWeb
The standard Wilson indexes combined in one database, covering all disciplines. With selected full-text.

Infotrac
Information on astronomy, religion, law, history, psychology, humanities, current events, sociology, communications and the general sciences. With selected full-text.

Subject databases: Check the <u>Research Resources</u> page.

Finding the full text of an article

Check our list of <u>electronic journals</u>, to find out if we have the article in either print or electronic format.

From the <u>library home page</u>, select "print and electronic journals" from Quick Information Links, or
From the <u>Research Resources</u> page, find the link under "General Sources."

How do you get personal help from a librarian? Ask at the Reference Desk, or contact:
<u>Margaret Guccione</u>
X6370

Tutorial available at: <u>http://www.goucher.edu/library/ulansey_fa02.html</u>

ONLINE LIBRARY TUTORIAL

Information comes in many forms: books, magazines, newspapers, scholarly journals, the Internet. During the next four years, you will often be required to find information to complete various research projects. In fact, you will need information to deal with situations that arise at many times throughout your life. That is why it is important for you to learn to recognize when you need information and to know how to find the appropriate type of information. This tutorial is the first of several steps in North Central College Library Services Information Literacy Program designed to help you master the process of information gathering.

The next page is a worksheet that you will fill out as you work through this tutorial. Use a topic that is of interest to you in working your way through the tutorial. Please click on the link below and print out the worksheet. Continue to click on the forward links as you work your way through this tutorial. Enter your answers to the questions posed in each step of the tutorial on the worksheet.

Please note: If you are completing this tutorial from **off-campus,** you will be asked for your library ID, which is your 14 digit North Central College Student ID number, located under the bar code at the bottom of your student ID card.

If you have any questions or problems completing this tutorial, please feel free to contact Rosemary Henders, Instructional Services Librarian, at 637-5707, or by e-mail.

<u>Worksheet</u>

<u>The Research Question</u>
<u>Finding Information</u>
<u>Dewey Decimal Classification System</u>
<u>Reference Books</u>
<u>Finding a Book</u>
<u>Finding an Article</u>
<u>Finding a Web Site</u>
<u>Review</u>

This file was last updated: Wednesday, 28-Aug-2002 14:48:02 CDT

NORTH CENTRAL COLLEGE LIBRARY SERVICES
ONLINE LIBRARY TUTORIAL
WORKSHEET

1. The Research Question:

State your research question below. Be as specific as possible.

Now identify the "key words" in your research question. Key words are the important words that identify what it is you are looking for. Enter keywords here:

2. Dewey Decimal Classification System

What general Dewey number do you think would be assigned to materials on your topic?

3. Reference Books

Encyclopedia Title:

Volume:

Page:

Title of article:

Does the article have a bibliography? yes/no

4. Finding a Book

Title of the book you have selected:

Author:

Places of publication:

Publisher:

Date of publication:

North Central College

Call number:

List several of the Library of Congress Subject Headings assigned to this book: (There may only be one. You need not list more than three.)

5. Finding an Article

Database searched:

Title of article:

Author:

Title of periodical:

Date:

Volume:

Page:

6. Finding a Web Site

Which directory did you use?

What is the title of the web site you selected?

What is the URL of the web site you selected?

7. Review

Did you succeed in locating information that answers your research question in each of these formats?

1. Overview article in reference book? yes/no
2. Book? yes/no
3. Periodical article? yes/no
4. Web site? yes/no

Student Name_____

NORTH CENTRAL COLLEGE LIBRARY SERVICES
ONLINE LIBRARY TUTORIAL
THE RESEARCH QUESTION

Before beginning any research project, it is important to define what information you are looking for. For the purposes of this tutorial, use a topic of interest to you in completing the exercises below.

The first step in doing research is to formulate a research question. It is often helpful to try to answer the questions Who? What? When? Where? Why? as you begin this process.

> *Example: If my topic is drug abuse, my research question might be "Should marijuana be legalized in the United States for medical purposes?"*

State your research question on your worksheet. Be as specific as possible.

Now identify the "key words" in your research question. Key words are the important words that identify what it is you are looking for.

> *Example: In the above research question, the keywords would be: marijuana, legalize, medical purposes, United States*

Enter keywords on your worksheet.

Now you are ready to begin your research.

Tutorial available at:
http://www.noctrl.edu/library_ncc/help/english115_125web/index.shtml

Pre-Test

- **Test Your Knowledge**
  (use Internet Explorer 4.0+)

Lessons

1. The Production of Knowledge
   A. *The Politics of Research*
2. The Organization of Knowledge
3. Defining Your Research Topic
4. Using Electronic Resources
5. Using Print Resources
6. Citing Your Sources
7. Intellectual Freedom & Censorship

Quizzes

Must use a 4.0+ Internet Explorer

1. Lesson 1 Quiz
2. Lesson 2 Quiz
3. Lesson 3 Quiz
4. Lesson 4 Quiz
5. Lesson 5 Quiz
6. Lesson 6 Quiz
7. Lesson 7 Quiz

Assignments

Print off the assignments and attempt to answer all the questions. You will use the *Developing a Research Strategy* assignment as a basis for all the other assignments.

Introduction & Use Guidelines

This **Tutorial** is a self-paced instructional resource designed to assist Northern State University students master information literacy skills. The **Pre-Test** will help you assess your knowledge before you begin the **Tutorial**. The **Lessons** provide detailed instruction and are the core of the **Tutorial**. To take full advantage of the **Tutorial** you should read each lesson before you attempt to take the quizzes, do the assignments or the database exercises. There is a **Quiz** for each lesson which allows you to test your understanding of the information presented . The **Assignments** allow you to apply what you have learned in the lessons by performing actual tasks. **Guided Exercises** provide hands-on searching experience using the Internet and electronic databases.

In order to take the quizzes you must be using either Netscape Communicator 4.0 or higher, or Internet Explorer 4.0 or higher. To check the version of your browser go to the "Help" option on the menu bar and select either "About Netscape," "About Communicator," or "About Internet Explorer." If you are using a browser below 4.0 you will need to download and install a new version. You can download a new version of Netscape for free by going to the Netscape download page. You can download a new version of Internet Explorer for free by going to Internet Explorer download page.

To read the assignments, handouts, and sample exam your browser must have Adobe Acrobat Reader as a plug-in. To find out if you have the Acrobat Reader plug-in simply click on any of these documents. If you have the plug-in the document will appear in your web browser. If you don't have the plug-in it

1. Developing a Research Strategy
   A. Research Strategy Example
2. Yahoo!
3. Google
4. Library Catalog
5. General Magazines
6. Encyclopedias
7. Statistics

Database Exercises

Internet

- Browsing Yahoo!
- Searching Yahoo!
- Google

Catalogs and Indexes

- Library Catalog
- Infotrac - Expanded Academic ASAP
- ERIC

won't work. To get the plug-in go to http://www.adobe.com/products/acrobat/readermain.html and download the software. Once you download the software you will need to install it before you can view the documents.

Helpful Handouts

- Dewey Decimal Classification
- Library of Congress Classification
- What is a Scholarly Journal? Chart
- Evaluation of Web AND Print Resources
- SDLN Button Chart

Last updated: August 20, 2002.
The Tutorial was updated and revised for use at Northern State University by Jennifer Campbell.
©2002 Northern State University

This tutorial was created and written by Thomas W. Eland, Instructor/Librarian at Minneapolis Community & Technical College. All material is copyrighted and cannot be duplicated without the express permission of Thomas Eland.
©1999 Minneapolis Community & Technical College
The *Tutorial* was created using Dreamweaver 3, HoTMetaL PRO 6, and PaintShop PRO 7 software

Defining Your Research Topic & Starting Your Search

Lesson 3

Navigation Menu

- **Introduction**
- Designing a strategy
- Determining use
- Quiz

Defining Your Research Topic and Starting Your Search

The difference between a beginning researcher and an expert is in the amount of time spent in defining the topic. Expert researchers take the necessary time to think about what it is they are trying to find and put their requests into terms that work within the structures of the library and online information systems.

The time you spend defining your research topic is well worth the effort. In order to locate information in library databases or on the Internet you must clearly understand what you are looking for and know how your topic fits into other areas of knowledge and research.

David Novak makes a very good point in his "The Information Research FAQ: 100 Pages of Search Techniques, Tactics and Theory," when he states:

The information sphere is very large and rather confusing. Each item of information has aspects of authenticity, accuracy, reliability, and bias. Information comes in many formats: interviews, books, articles, statistics. We learn about information from many sources: literature, discussion, resource lists, experience. There are also personal issues: budget, time, depth and purpose.

With all this to think about, we must be very careful about each question we ask. This issue is vital once we start an article search, and can easily mean the difference between 5 concise articles, and hundreds of general articles. The essence of our question is the manner with which we approach the information sphere. The question directs our efforts.

One key is to treat searching as an art, much like painting or photography. The true mark of an artist, and the primary step wanna-be artists miss, is visualizing what you want before you begin.

The following sections of the *Tutorial* will provide you with ideas on how to begin the research process.

Defining Your Research Topic & Starting Your Search

Lesson 3

Navigation Menu

- Introduction
- **Designing a strategy**
- Determining use
- Quiz

Designing a Strategy to Locate Information

Choosing a topic

Often the hardest part of writing a research paper is selecting the right topic. A good topic should sustain your interest over the time that it will take to do your research and write your paper. It should be meaningful to you personally, raise questions that have no simple answers, and provide you with an opportunity to expand your knowledge through critical assessment of various points of view.

Determining if your topic is too broad or too narrow

No matter what topic you choose, it must have a focus. Many topics are too broad or too loosely defined at first. Decide which aspect of a topic interests you most and identify the **keywords** used to describe your topic before you start to look for background information.

Most research topics can be approached from different angles. For example, if you were writing a paper on animal rights you would probably want to focus your paper on a specific aspect of animal rights. The aspect you choose will lead you to different sources. For instance, focusing on the moral and ethical issues raised by large corporate farms would take you in a different direction than if you chose to write about the ethical use of animals in medical research. And if you chose to write about the use of animals in religion, you would look in completely different places for the information.

Thinking of terminology that you can use in locating information on your topic

To help you narrow your topic, you could look for keywords or headings in the indexes of encyclopedias, in periodical indexes, or in the table of contents of books covering your topic. All of these sources can provide you with terms that will aid you in your search.

State your topic as a question

Often it is helpful to state your topic in the form of a question and then isolate the key ideas or concepts. For example, instead of saying that you want to do a paper on "genetics," pose the topic in the form of a specific question: "What are the scientific and ethical issues of reproduction research, specifically those related to cloning?" Or, "Is research into the idea of splitting off cells from embryos to clone human beings ethically acceptable?" The keywords contained in these statements will then form the basis for search terms you can use in the online catalog or appropriate periodical indexes. Other questions to ask yourself include the following:

- "What is the main idea of my paper?"
- "What specific ideas am I trying to describe or prove?"
- "What academic discipline does my topic fit into?"
- "What specific aspect of the topic do I wish to consider?"

Determine the particular aspect of a topic that interests you

Most topics can be examined from different angles. To be successful in looking for information you need to know what aspect of a topic you are looking for. Do you want to know about the ethical, the social, the

political, or the religious aspect of the topic?
The particular aspect of the topic that you
choose will affect how you search for the
information. For example, you would use very
different resources to look for information on
abortion from a religious or ethical point of
view than you would to look for information
on abortion from a medical or health point of
view.

Finding background information

Encyclopedias, dictionaries, and textbooks
can all provide you with a helpful overview of
a particular subject, and frequently you will
find a useful bibliography at the end of the
article, entry, or chapter. The bibliography
will lead you to other books and articles that
will be helpful to you in doing your research.
Bibliographies are one of a researchers best
friends.

QUIZ 3

Select the appropriate answer, or answers, for each question . You will get immediate feedback on the true and false and single answer multiple choice questions. For the multiple choice questions with more than one right answer you must press the submit button when you are done. If you pick the wrong choices simply press the reset button and try again. Good luck.

1. One of the most difficult aspects of writing a research paper is determining how narrow to focus your topic.

⭕ True ⭕ False

2. One way to help focus your research paper is to state your topic in the form of a question and isolate the key ideas or concepts. Other questions to ask yourself before you begin your research include?

☐ What is the main idea of my paper?

☐ What specific ideas am I trying to describe or prove?

☐ What academic disciplines does my topic fit into?

☐ What specific aspects of the topic do I wish to consider?

3. The majority of published information is now available online.

⭕ True ⭕ False

4. The advantages of searching for information online include?

☐ it is usually faster, especially when you search across multiple years

☐ you can combine search terms

☐ the information is updated more frequently

☐ the information is more accurate

5. The disadvantages of searching for information online includes?

☐ you often get an enormous number of search results, especially when using web search engines

☐ you get a number of false hits, i.e., items that contain your keywords but do not match your topic

☐ you always have to pay extra for the information

---

6. The advantages of searching for information using print indexes include?

☐ they provide subject cross references to other related topics

☐ the information is more accurate

☐ they index material published prior to the invention of full-text online indexes

---

Tutorial available at: http://lib.northern.edu/infolit/tablesversion/home.htm

LIBRARY TUTORIAL

INTRODUCTION SOURCE MATERIALS CITATIONS BOOKS

ARTICLES SEARCHING DATABASES WWW GLOSSARY

INTRODUCTION

This library tutorial was developed to introduce you to essential library skills that will contribute to your success as a student. It was designed to familiarize you with fundamental concepts that will empower you to efficiently and effectively locate, evaluate, and use information. Because there is so much information available from so many different sources, it is often difficult to know what sources to use, when to use them, and how to use them. Learning these basic library skills, becoming familiar with the sources and services available at your library, and understanding the information process will help you become a better student and informed citizen. You will be on your way to becoming information literate.

Navigation of the tutorial is easy. Just click on any of the chapters listed at the top of the tutorial to go to that chapter. Some of the chapters have several sections within that chapter. After you have read a section just click the BACK button on the toolbar to get back to the beginning of the tutorial.

At the end of each chapter there is a link to a PRACTICE page for that chapter. Each practice page has several Practice Exercises that will reinforce what you just learned in that chapter.

A great place to start is with the
LIBRARY TOUR

SOURCE MATERIALS

Primary and secondary sources are used when collecting information for a research project.

Primary Sources

A primary source is firsthand testimony about a topic under investigation. It records events as witnessed and often enables the researcher to get as close to the truth as possible. Primary sources include interviews, manuscripts, diaries, letters, and speeches.

University of Montevallo

Secondary Sources

Secondary sources describe, interpret, and analyze primary sources and are one step removed from the event. Scholars use primary sources to develop secondary sources. Books, encyclopedia articles, and scholarly journal articles are considered secondary sources.

Select primary and secondary sources when you have the opportunity to do so.

Several examples of primary and secondary sources include:

ART
Primary Source: Guernica by Pablo Picasso
Secondary Source: A web site about the painting **Guernica**

HISTORY
Primary Source: Declaration of Independence
Secondary Source: A book listed in the **Library Catalog** about the Declaration of Independence

LITERATURE
Primary Source: The Raven by Edgar Allen Poe
Secondary Source: A scholarly journal article from **MLA International Bibliography** about The Raven

THEATER
Primary Source: A live performance of "Les Miserables"
Secondary Source: An article about **"Les Miserables"**.

PRACTICE ~ SOURCE MATERIALS

CITATIONS

How to read a citation

Being information literate includes the ability to read and write citations accurately. The only way to learn this is by reading and writing citations often. At first you will have to follow a style manual, but you will quickly learn the parts of a citation and how read and write them. Then you will only have to refer to a style manual for the less common types of sources.

A citation describes the material used for research. The main parts of the citation include the author's name, title, and publication information. The parts of a citation are listed in a particular order based on an accepted standard such as *MLA* (Modern Language Association) or *APA* (American Psychological Association) which enables the reader to recognize the source. In other words, by looking at a citation you should be able to recognize what it is, and then know where and how to locate it.

Practice ~ Source Materials

PRACTICE EXERCISE 1

List five primary sources.

PRACTICE EXERCISE 2

List five corresponding secondary sources.

PRACTICE EXERCISE 3

You are doing a research paper about the history of genetics. You recently watched a television show about genetics. The man who discovered DNA, Dr. James D. Watson, was interviewed. You want to use something he said in the interview in your research paper. Is the television show and interview with Dr. Watson a primary or secondary source?

PRACTICE EXERCISE 4

How many primary sources and secondary sources did you use in your last research paper?

Tutorial available at:
http://www.montevallo.edu/library/Instruction&Research/LibraryTutorial/default.shtm

Encouraging Student Inquiry:
The Role of Library Research and Information Skills
A Resource Page for Faculty

- Library Research & Information Skills Program Proposal
- Library Skills Workshops for First Year Students Proposal
- Library Research & Information Skills Competencies
- Designing Research Intensive Assignments
- Examples of Research Intensive Assignments
- Arranging Library Instruction for Your Students

Proposed Program for Library & Information Skills

During spring semester of 2002, the Libraries received a PETE grant to host three lunch meetings for a Faculty Focus Group to discuss strategies to encourage student inquiry with library research and information skills. Faculty participants represented a variety of departments, including English, Religion, Rhetoric and Communication, History, Biology, Economics, Political Science, Women's Studies, Physics, Psychology and Music.

The group's primary goal was to discuss "what do/should students know about identifying appropriate information resources for research?" and to ask for faculty input in three areas, each progressing from the one before:

1. What are the core library and information research competencies that faculty think every University of Richmond student should master?
2. What curricular structures and/or pedagogical techniques are most effective in teaching students these competencies?
3. What strategies do faculty recommend to assure effective and widespread adoption of needed changes in curricular structures and/or pedagogical techniques?

Discussion themes included:

- Lack of student use and understanding of primary resources
- Identifying and finding appropriate secondary sources
- Student over reliance on the Web for research
- Lack of student passion for research
- Evaluating information for quality and reliability
- Integration of information-seeking skills into coursework
- Importance of framing assignments so that students learn the steps of research
- How to teach both basic and advanced competencies of information fluency

At the third and final meeting in March, the group agreed upon a library and information research skills program which includes the following components:

- **Library and Information Skills Workshops for First Year Students**

    Develop a workshop model for first year students to teach basic competencies of using the library and finding appropriate information resources. This workshop model would consist of an introductory online tutorial, an hour and a half workshop during fall semester and an hour and a half workshop during spring semester. Both the online tutorial and workshops would be required pass/fail credits and would work in a similar manner to the Wellness Requirement. The program would be administered and taught by librarians. For more details, see Proposal for Library and Information Skills Workshops for First Year Students

Implement "research intensive" assignments in general education courses to reinforce basic research skills.

Create a web site that offers examples of research intensive assignments that have been used successfully by faculty and librarians. General Education instructors will be encouraged to develop "research intensive" assignments to reinforce the basic skills that are taught in the Library and Information Skills workshops.

- **Provide Student Research Fellows to Serve as Peer Tutors**

  A grant from the Associated Colleges of the South will make student Research Fellows available to faculty as peer tutors by training them via a 3 credit course and paying them to work with teaching faculty and librarians to assist other students with research assignments in particular courses. The training course would be taught primarily by librarians and would include guest lectures by faculty and Academic Technologies staff. Courses in our general education curriculum would be targeted for placement of the Research Fellows. This program would be analogous to the university's current Writing Fellows, who take a course covering advanced composition and tutoring skills, and are then assigned to faculty who have requested a Fellow.

- **Integrate advanced research skills into the curriculum of academic departments.**

Individual departments will have the opportunity to apply for PETE grants to develop an Advanced Research Skills workshop with librarians to integrate specialized skills into upper-level curriculum that would benefit the students who are majoring in a particular field of academic study. This will assure faculty that students graduate with a working knowledge of the major databases, journals and other reference tools in their discipline.

LIST: Library & Information Skills Tutorial

Module 1: Virtual Library Tour
Learn the locations and services of all campus libraries.

Module 2: Starting Your Research
Take a "tour" of the library web page and learn how to get answers fast.

Module 3: Finding Articles
See how *Expanded Academic ASAP* can help you find journal articles.

Module 4: Finding Books
Learn how to find books using the Library of Congress classification system.

Module 5: Using the Web Effectively
Learn what to look for in a reliable Web site.

Module 6: Plagiarism, Copyright, and Citing Sources
When and how can you use other people's work?

Module 7: Computing Services at the University of Richmond
Where to find computing resources.

Module 8: Finding Help
Meet the 10 most effective information resources in the UR Libraries.

Module 9: Take the Quiz!

LIST: Plagiarism, Copyright and Citing Sources

What Is Copyright And How Does It Affect You?

You probably know that Napster was forced to alter its service because it was found guilty of "copyright infringement." What you also need to know is that: · Copyright is a form of protection provided by the laws of the United States (title 17, U.S. Code) to the authors of "original works of authorship," including literary, dramatic, musical, artistic, and certain other intellectual works that are considered "intellectual property."

This protection gives copyright holders the exclusive right to reproduce, distribute, perform, or display their work, to create derivative works, or to authorize other people to do any of these things.

The writers of song lyrics and scores and the performers all have copyright to their contributions to the musical recordings being downloaded from the Internet, or they have assigned it to some other authority (like the music recording companies).

LIST: Plagiarism, Copyright and Citing Sources

What Works Are Protected?

Copyright protects creative works that have been written or recorded in any way, including

· literary, musical, dramatic, pictorial, graphic, and sculptural works;
· motion pictures and other audiovisual works;
· sound recordings, in any medium.

Even personal letters (including email messages) are the intellectual property of the writer and cannot be published without permission. These categories have become broader as technology develops.

For example, the reason you can't just make a copy of a computer software program is that it is considered a "literary work"; designs, drawings, and photographs you find on the Internet are considered pictorial or graphic works. Even without official registration, the creator automatically has a right to his or her intellectual property, but if you create something you want to protect, it is a good idea to register it.

Copyright, Plagiarism, and Citing Sources

These **four** questions will help you test your understanding of copyright and plagiarism issues. Use the arrow buttons to navigate.

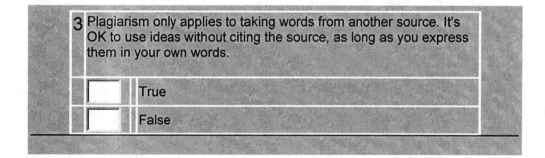

1 Copyright protects works of fiction, but not nonfiction, because they're just facts.

| | True |
| | False |

When people put something on the Internet, it's OK to copy and use it any way you want. That's why it's there.

| | True |
| | False |

3 Plagiarism only applies to taking words from another source. It's OK to use ideas without citing the source, as long as you express them in your own words.

| | True |
| | False |

4 When you use a magazine article from an electronic database, like Expanded Academic Index, you have to cite the electronic form, not the print form.

| | True |
| | False |

Tutorial available at: http://oncampus.richmond.edu/is/library/list/

Credits

Rhonda Gonzales, Assistant Professor of Library Services, University of Southern Colorado created InfoTrail during the Summer and Fall Semesters of 2001. The project was completed in conjunction with and with the support of the University's Instructional Technology Center. This center is funded by a Title III Grant from the U.S. Department of Education.

The project took approximately 6 months to complete. Rhonda primarily used Macromedia Fireworks and Dreamweaver to create the tutorial. In addition, she used Quicktime Virtual Reality and Macromedia Flash to create animations.

Many thanks to Sam Ebersole, Geri Koncilja, and Marge Vorndam in the Instructional Technology Center for help with numerous questions and especially for helping me figure out the MAC!

Goals

The InfoTrail Tutorial will help you develop your <u>Information Literacy</u> Skills.

After completing the InfoTrail tutorial, you will be able to:

1. Clearly identify your information needs.
2. Identify good sources of information.
3. Find your way around the USC Library.
4. Use the Wolf Den to find books and journal titles in the USC collection.
5. Use Academic Search Premier to find journal articles.
6. Find and evaluate relevant information on the Internet.

Directions

1. From the menu on the left, select the module you wish to complete.

2. Click on the paw prints at the bottom of each screen to move through the tutorial or click on "Follow the InfoTrail".

3. First, take the short Pre-Test before you start the tutorial. At the end, you'll take the quiz again. This will help us determine whether InfoTrail has helped you learn how to use the USC Library.

4. You can work through the modules in order, or you can jump around, but it may be most helpful to start with "Tracking Down Information".

5. If you run across specialized terms you are not familiar with, consult InfoTrail's Glossary by clicking on "Glossary" in the left hand menu.

6. Complete the activities and exercises as you go along. **If an activity appears in a new browser window, just close that window to return to the tutorial!**

7. If you are completing the tutorial as part of a class, your tests and assignments will be emailed to your professor. **It would also be a good idea to print out copies for yourself to keep. If you are asked to do InfoTrail again in another class, you'll already have it done!**

8. Have Fun!

Pre-Test

Tracking Down Information

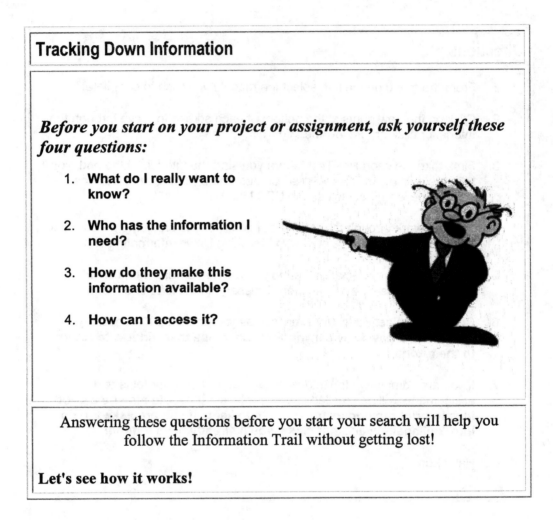

Before you start on your project or assignment, ask yourself these four questions:

1. **What do I really want to know?**

2. **Who has the information I need?**

3. **How do they make this information available?**

4. **How can I access it?**

Answering these questions before you start your search will help you follow the Information Trail without getting lost!

Let's see how it works!

InfoTrail

1. Tracking Down Information:

What Do I Really Want to Know?

By focusing your topic, you will help focus your searching and save yourself time and energy! No one wants to waste time or energy do they?

Let's say you are interested in the Internet. If you start searching databases and search engines for **"internet"** you will find millions of sources. Way too many!

What is it about the Internet that interests you? Are you interested in how businesses use the Internet? Are you following the Napster controversy?

Be Specific!

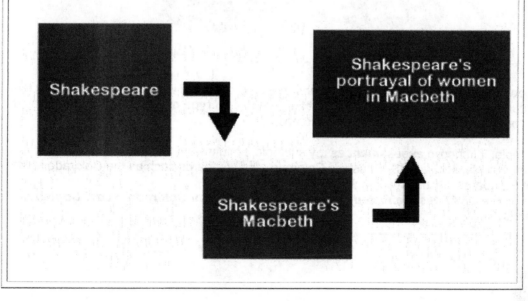

Focus Your Topic

The first step to focusing your topic is to brainstorm. Think about all the possible questions you might ask about your topic. What are all the issues related to your topic. Try jotting them down like the diagram below.

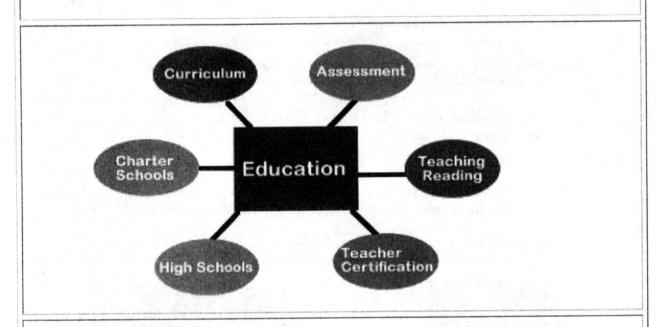

Now choose the subtopic that interests you the most. What do you want to know about this topic? What is your question? **This question should not be a yes or no type of question**, but rather a question that explores relationships or examines outcomes.

For example, if I choose *assessment* as my subtopic, I might want to explore the relationship between assessment tools, such as CSAP tests in Colorado, and standards such as the Colorado Model Content Standards. My question might be:
How have the CSAP tests effected students' achievement of Colorado Model Content Standards?

 Assignment 1: Choosing and Focusing Your Topic

NOTE: English 101 students who are working through InfoTrail as part of a class must complete all assignments!

Library Assignment 1- Choosing and Focusing Your Topic

NOTE: If you are completing InfoTrail for a class, you must complete all the assignments. When you click the "submit" button at the bottom of the assignment, it will be emailed to your professor. If you wish you may also print out the assignment to hand in. It is a good idea to keep a copy for yourself.

Purpose:
To define an appropriately focused research topic and identify useful keywords for that topic.

Items marked with an * are required fields!
Top of Form

*Select your Instructor from the list: [Instructor Name ▼]

*Select your class from the list: [Class Name ▼]

*Your Name: [ ]

*Your Email: [ ]

1. **Choose a topic from the following list or use a topic of your own choosing if you have something definite in mind.** At this point, you should be thinking of concepts or general topics, but if your topic is too broad, like "violence" for example, you should try to narrow it to a particular focus.
Choose one of the topics below or type in your own.

○ Women in the American West   ○ Technology in education

○ Ethics of Violence   ○ Teens and violence

○ Religion and Culture   ○ Edgar Allen Poe

[ ] (fill in your topic)

2. **List some subtopics or different aspects of this topic that you might investigate:**

3. **Choose the subtopic listed above that you would like to research and type it in the box.**

[ ]

4. What about this topic do you want to find out? Be specific. Type a question that expresses your research focus. For example: "What impact has technology had on education?" **This should not be a yes or no question, but an open-ended type of question.** If you are having trouble with this, see your instructor or the Reference Librarian for help.

Type your research question here.

5. Read the question you wrote in number two. Which <u>key words</u> from that question express the most relevant concepts in your question? Which key words would probably be present in the title or subject of a source that answered your question? (In the case of my question, "technology", "impact", and "education" would all be likely to be present in a source that really answered my question.) **List the two or three key words from your question that are the most relevant to your topic.**

6. Can you think of any alternative terms for your key words? (In my case, I might search under "computers" instead of "technology", or "effect" instead of "impact".

List your alternative key words here.

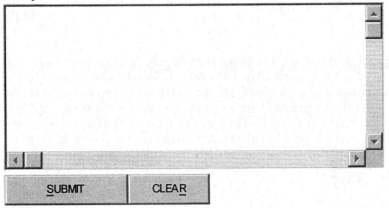

Bottom of Form

Tutorial available at: http://library.uscolo.edu/infotrail/infotrail.html

| XU HOME | SEARCH | XU CONTACT INFO |

University Library

xu.tutor > home

Instructions
Table of Contents
Defining the Question
Identifying Resources
Improving a Search
Evaluating Websites
Glossary
> xu.tutor Home
Libraries Home

Welcome to xu.tutor!

Xu.tutor was created with an Ameritech Partnership Award to help you in your research. Proceed through each page of xu.tutor by clicking the **next >>** button.

Defining the Questio

This tutorial will help you focus your research topic and identify its key concepts.

Identifying Resource

This tutorial will help you choose the most useful resources for your research.

Improving a Search

This tutorial will help you formulate an initial search strategy and provide additional strategies for improving your search.

Evaluating Websites

This tutorial will help you locate reliable information on the World Wide Web.

<< back

next >>

Xavier University Library
3800 Victory Parkway
Cincinnati, OH 45207-5211

Last updated: 11/06/2002 12:21 PM
Comments: xututor@xu.edu
Help: 513 745-4808

University Library

xu.tutor > improving a search

Instructions
Table of Contents
Defining the Question
Identifying Resources
> Improving a Search
Evaluating Websites
Glossary
xu.tutor Home
Libraries Home

Description:

This tutorial will help you formulate your search strategy using **Boolean operators**, **truncation**, and **limits**. It will also provide additional strategies for broadening and narrowing in your search.

Content:

1. Narrowing and broadening a search
2. Combining key concepts in a search
3. Understanding Boolean operators
4. Using the OR operator
5. Using the AND operator
6. Using the NOT operator
7. Using truncation to broaden a search
8. Using limits to narrow a search
9. Evaluating search results

<< back   next >>

Xavier University Library
3800 Victory Parkway
Cincinnati, OH 45207-5211

Last updated: 08/02/2002 11:59 AM
Comments: xututor@xu.edu
Help: 513 745-4808

University Library

xu.tutor > improving a search

Instructions

Table of Contents

Defining the Question

Identifying Resources

> Improving a Search

Evaluating Websites

Glossary

xu.tutor Home

Libraries Home

1. Narrowing and broadening a search

To formulate a good **search strategy** you must combine the **key concepts** identified in your research question. The way key concepts are combined directly influences the results of your search. Combinations that broaden a search increase results while combinations that narrow a search decrease results. **Example**

Combining	Effect	Results
Similar terms in a key concept	Broaden	Increase
Different key concepts	Narrow	Decrease

<< back   next >>

Xavier University Library
3800 Victory Parkway
Cincinnati, OH 45207-5211

Last updated: 08/02/2002 11:25 AM
Comments: xututor@xu.edu
Help: 513 745-4808

University Library

xu.tutor > improving a search

2. Combining key concepts in a search

To demonstrate combining key concepts in a search, use the research question, key concepts, and additional terms from the first tutorial:

What determines the number of Ohio high school students who go on to college?

Key concepts	Additional terms	Type of term
High school students	High school seniors	Narrower term
	Students	Broader term
	Teenagers	Related term
	Adolescents	Related term
	Teens	Related term
Ohio	Cleveland	Narrower term
	Cincinnati	Narrower term
	Columbus	Narrower term
	Midwest	Broader term
College	Community colleges	Narrower term
	Universities	Broader term
	Higher Education	Related term

Documents in our search results should include all three key concepts. However, we may use selected additional terms to increase (broaden) or decrease (narrow) our search results.

<< back   **next >>**

Xavier University Library
3800 Victory Parkway
Cincinnati, OH 45207-5211

Last updated: 08/16/2002 4:24 PM
Comments: xututor@xu.edu
Help: 513 745-4808

University Library

xu.tutor > improving a search

Instructions
Table of Contents
Defining the Question
Identifying Resources
> Improving a Search
Evaluating Websites
Glossary
xu.tutor Home
Libraries Home

3. Understanding Boolean operators

Use the **Boolean operators** AND, OR, or NOT to combine terms and key concepts.

Operator	Effect	Results	Terms included
OR	Broadens	Increases	Any
AND	Narrows	Decreases	All
NOT	Narrows	Decreases	All but NOT term

<< back   next >>

Xavier University Library
3800 Victory Parkway
Cincinnati, OH 45207-5211

Last updated: 01/08/2002 11:54 AM
Comments: xututor@xu.edu
Help: 513 745-4808

Instructions
Table of Contents
Defining the Question
Identifying Resources
> Improving a Search
Evaluating Websites
Glossary
xu.tutor Home
Libraries Home

4. Using the OR operator

In our search example, the OR operator is used to combine terms that are equivalent or that have similar meanings; for example, *high school students* OR *high school seniors*. This will result in documents that discuss either high school students or high school seniors. Results are represented by the yellow areas in the diagram shown below.

High School Students OR High School Seniors = 1,610

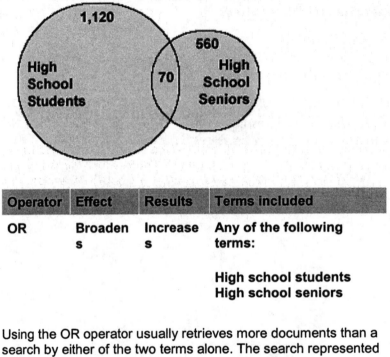

Operator	Effect	Results	Terms included
OR	Broadens	Increases	Any of the following terms:
			High school students High school seniors

Using the OR operator usually retrieves more documents than a search by either of the two terms alone. The search represented in the diagram above would retrieve about 1,610 unique documents. In this example there are some documents that discuss both topics, about 70, and these duplicates are counted only once. Therefore, when a search produces too few documents, combine similar terms with the OR operator.

<< back   next >>

Xavier University Library
3800 Victory Parkway
Cincinnati, OH 45207-5211

Last updated: 10/09/2002 8:51 AM
Comments: xututor@xu.edu
Help: 513 745-4808

XAVIER

University Library

xu.tutor > improving a search

XuTutor Quiz: Improving a search

Instructions
Table of Contents
Defining the Question
Identifying Resources
Improving a Search
Evaluating Websites
Glossary
xu.tutor Home
Libraries Home

Fill in your personal info, take the quiz, and then click the "submit quiz" button at the bottom of the page to send it to your instructor(s). If your instructor is not on the list, choose "no instructor" and after you submit the quiz, print out the page of results.

Your Name: [First and Last]

Your E-mail address: [you@xavier.e]

Instuctor [No Instructor ▼]

Course number-section [Not in a Class ▼]

1. The **OR** Boolean operator

   ○ Narrows a search

   ○ Broadens a search

   ○ Decreases results

2. The **AND** Boolean operator

   ○ Narrows a search

   ○ Broadens a search

   ○ Increases results

3. The **NOT** Boolean operator

   ○ Narrows a search

   ○ Broadens a search.

   ○ Increases results.

4. In the tutorial examples for the Boolean OR operator, when High School Students were combined with High School Seniors using OR,:

    ○ Both terms were included

    ○ There were more results

    ○ The search was broader than using one term by itself

    ○ All of the above.

5. In the tutorial examples for the Boolean AND operator, when High School Students/Seniors were combined with Ohio using AND:

    ○ Both terms were included

    ○ There were fewer results

    ○ The search was narrower than using one term by itself

    ○ All of the above.

6. In the tutorial examples for the Boolean NOT operator, when Three Musketeers was combined with Candy using NOT:

    ○ Candy was not included

    ○ There were fewer results

    ○ The search was narrower than using one term by itself

    ○ All of the above.

7. Topic: What is the effect of computer technology in schools? In your keyword search in ERIC using truncation **"comput$"** as a method of broadening your results, check below the terms which were searched

    ○ Computer

    ○ Computer uses in education

    ○ Computer assisted instruction

    ○ Computer-assisted testing

    ○ All of the above

8. Topic: Is team-teaching beneficial for my child?
   If your search results are too large, check some of the methods
   to limit your search in the ERIC database. (check all that apply)

   ☐ Year From and To

   ☐ Educational level

   ☐ French language

   ☐ Audience

9. If you wish to broaden your search, which methods could you
   use?(check all that apply)

   ☐ Use OR Boolean operator

   ☐ Use AND Boolean operator

   ☐ Use Truncation

10. If you wish to narrow your search, which methods could you
    use?(check all that apply)

    ☐ Use OR Boolean operator

    ☐ Use AND Boolean operator

    ☐ Use Limits

[Submit Quiz]

Tutorial available at: http://www.xavier.edu/library/xututor/

Documents:
Exercises

LIBRARY SEARCH WORKSHEET	C/I 11 A: BUSINESS ETHICS – OXYMORON OR EMPOWERMENT?

Name: _____ Date: _____

I. List a business ethics topic about which you want to know more:

   _____

II. List three or four possible terms that may help you to search about your topic:

   _____   _____

   _____   _____

   _____   _____

III. Use Google's basic search to conduct a search on your business ethics topic, such as the lawsuits over the Ford Pinto. How many websites did you find? _____
Select a website from the first page and answer the following questions: Who put up the website? _____
When was the website last updated? _____
List some additional terms you might find helpful: _____

   _____

IV. Use Google's advanced search to conduct a search on your topic. First use the option "With All of the Words." How many websites did you find? _____
Next limit the search to "exact phrase" How many websites did you find?
_____ Next redo the search and limit the File Format to "Adobe Acrobat PDF" (.pdf). How many websites did you find? _____ Do these websites appear more relevant to your search than those you found from your first search?

   _____

V. From the information learned from these and any other websites searched, go back and use Google to construct a more sophisticated search. Find a website and evaluate it by answering the following questions:

   What is the name and URL of the Website: _____

   _____

   A. Authority:

      1. Who developed the page (Is it signed?)? _____

      2. Is the author qualified to write about the topic? _____ How can you tell?

         _____

   B. Bias:

      1. Does the author express a particular point of view? _____

         _____

2. Might the author (s) background or perspective influence his/or objectivity?

   _____

3. Is the page designed to influence your opinion? _____

4. Is there advertising on the page? _____

C. Currency:

   1. Is the page dated? _____

   2. When was the last time it was updated? _____

D. Details: Did you find any details that might be out of date or inaccurate?

   _____

E. Exposure:

   1. What topics are covered? _____

   2. Are there topics covered not found in other sources you have located
      elsewhere?

      _____

   3. Does the site provide links to more in-depth material?

      _____

VI.   Correctly cite this website using the style you have chosen from <u>Electronic Styles</u>
      by Xia Li and Nancy B. Crane (on reserve). Remember, citation conventions vary
      from discipline to discipline and sometimes from journal to journal within a
      discipline.

Author/editor. (last update or copyright date). *Homepage Title* [Homepage of . . .],
[Online]. Available: URL [Access Date].

Maloney, C., Lichtblau, S. J., Karpook, N., & Arena-DeRosa, (2000, November 17-
last update). *Feline Reactions to Bearded Men* [Homepage of the Technology
Learning Center of the College of Education of the University of Central Arkansas],
[Online]. Available
http://www.uca.edu/divisions/academic/coe/tlc/TeachMe/instructor/session3/cat.pdf
[2002, September 2001]

_____

_____

_____

CI0011A-02-Arnold2-worksheet
September 24, 2002

Return this exercise to a Reference Librarian by October 25.
Name
Box Number

Humanities Professor

HUMANITIES LIBRARY EXERCISE

October 2002

Imagine that you are planning to write a paper comparing women's rights in Iran and Iraq. In this exercise you will look for both web sites and journal articles on this topic.

SEARCH FOR WEB SITES

Go to www.google.com

Select **Advanced Search.** This will give you more control over the results of your search than the simple Google search does.

Type **women's rights** (be sure to include the apostrophe) in the **with all of the words** box. This will look for the word **women's** and the word **rights** anywhere in the web page. Search.
How many results were found? _____

Return to **Advanced Search.** Delete your first search and type **women's rights** in the **exact phrase** box. Search.
How many results were found? _____

Leaving **women's rights** in the **exact phrase** box, now type **iran iraq** in the **at least one of the words** box. This will find sites with either the word Iran or the word Iraq. Search.
 How many results were found? _____

These three searches produced very different results. Which one do you think would be the most useful to you? _____ Why do you think so?

_____

Choose the site: *International Campaign for Defense of Women's Rights in Iran*
(http://www2.womensnet.org.za/news/show.cfm?news_id=367)
What is the date on this page? _____
Is an individual _____ or an organization _____ taking credit for this page?
What information can you find about the organization from the page or its links?

_____

What information can you find about the background or qualifications of the authors of this page?
_____

Does this page offer any evidence (footnotes, references to other sources of information) for the statements? _____

What do you think is the purpose of this page?
    Advocate a point of view _____
    Present scholarly information _____
    Sell something _____
    Entertain _____

Back up to the list of web sites found by your Google search.
Choose: A *Declaration of Women's Rights in Islamic Societies.*
(http://www.secularhumanism.org/library/fi/women-17_4.html)

When was this page last updated? _____
Can you tell who wrote this page? _____
Does it present their background or qualifications? _____

This is an article from an online magazine. What organization sponsors this magazine? _____
_____
Does the website lead you to more information about the organization? _____

What do you think is the purpose of this page?
    Advocate a point of view _____
    Present scholarly information _____
    Sell something _____
    Entertain _____

Back up to the list of web sites found by your Google search.

Choose: *Donna M Hughes.*
(http://www.uri.edu/artsci/wms/hughes/pubfund.htm)

Who is Donna M. Hughes? _____

Look at her article "Women and Reform in Iran." Does she give any evidence (footnotes, references) for her statements? _____

What do you think is the purpose of this page?
    Advocate a point of view _____
    Present scholarly information _____
    Sell something _____
    Entertain _____

Now that you have found research sources through both Google and Academic Search Elite:

Earlham College

What are the advantages of searching for information on the web via Google?

What are the disadvantages of Google?

What are the advantages of searching for articles with Academic Search Elite?

What are the disadvantages of Academic Search Elite?

Eckerd College

USING THE LIBRARY WEB PAGE
(www.eckerd.edu/library)

(Successful Completion Fulfills One Element of the Technological Proficiency Requirement)

Name: _____ Instructor:_____

SEARCHING FOR BOOKS

1) Look up the following book in the on-line Catalog (Search for it *"as a phrase"*):

Using the information provided, cite this record as you would in a bibliography for a research paper. For line A, use the MLA format. For line B, use APA format. See A Writer's Reference for examples of these formats.

A)

_____

_____

B)

_____

_____

2) Click on the **"Detailed Record"** Tab that appears just above the boldface title near the top of the record. Locate "Subject(s)."

A) Jot down the subject heading for use in question 4:

_____

B) Click on the first subject heading listed. How many **Titles** (in the **"Titles"** column) are listed under this subject heading? _____

C) What is the **title of the first book** listed under this heading (click on 1 in the "#" column to list titles)? _____

D) What is the book's location, call number, and status:_____
_____

3) What other terms might you use to search for information on this topic? Be creative.

_____

Return to the main Library Web Page. Click on "Catalog." **Select and circle two or more** of the terms you listed above. Enter these terms together in one of the "Catalog" search boxes. How many items are listed when you search these terms using the drop down menus:

"all of these" _____   "any of these" _____

If the terms you chose return zero results in both categories,
choose other terms (make sure we can readily identify them)
and re-run the search.

SEARCHING FOR MAGAZINE, JOURNAL, & NEWSPAPER ARTICLES

4) Go to the main "Library Web Page" and click on **"Databases"**.

Click on **"View Complete List"**.

Click on **"Expanded Academic"** and enter the password **0148700**.

Click on **"Connect to InfoTrac"**. Select and click on the icon for **"Expanded Academic ASAP"**

Click on **"Keyword Search"** in the left-hand column

Enter **the subject heading you identified in 2A** and click on **Search.**

A) How many articles are listed? _____

If no articles are listed, see a librarian.

B) Is the first article available in full-text in this database?   Yes   No

C) Using the **"Back"** button, return to your original InfoTrac search screen. Click the box marked **"refereed publications."** Run the search again. How many articles are listed? _____

D) **Record the first citation from the "refereed"** list using E) MLA style and F) APA style as described in **"Citing Electronic Information"** on the main Library Web Page. If no articles are listed in the "refereed" category, use the first citation from 4A.

E)

_____

_____

F)_____

_____

5) Return to the Main Library Web Page and click on **"E-Journals"**.

In the search box, **enter the title of the Journal you cited in 4E and 4F.** If you are unsure what the title of the journal is, ask a librarian.

Eckerd College

A) Is the article available in full-text in a database(s) other than InfoTrac?   Yes   No

B) If it is available in another database(s), list the database(s) here:

_____

C) Does the library currently subscribe to a print/microfilm version of this title?   Yes   No

What is its call number?

_____

Where are the current issues located?

_____

6) Go back to the main **"Library Web Page"**, click on **"Databases"**, and click on _____

Choose a database other than InfoTrac from the list that you think might be useful in searching for information on topics covered in your class.

Which database did you choose?   _____

Using terms of your own choosing, conduct a search in this database on a topic related to your class and **attach a one page print out of the results** (not an article), to this assignment. If you get no results on your first try, select other terms or another database and re-run the search.

SEARCHING OTHER LIBRARY CATALOGS

7) Go back to the main Library Web Page and click on **"Beyond Eckerd"**

Select **"USF Web LUIS"** (first link under **"Search other Library Catalogs"**).

Highlight **"Title"** in the left-hand menu; then enter the title of the book from part 1 of this assignment (the one provided for you). Click on **"Submit Search."**

Is the book available in a USF Library?   Yes   No

Which one? Tampa _____   St. Pete _____   Sarasota _____Other _____

WHEN IN DOUBT, ASK A LIBRARIAN
WE'RE WAITING FOR YOUR
QUESTIONS

Topic: **"Sports Drinks"** such as Gatorade or AllSport. Together you and your partner will locate information on this topic.

You will write at least 2-3 paragraphs using information that you find as you search periodicals, books, and the web. You will note the pros and cons of the product(s), including what the company/author claims and what research says. When you have a choice of products you may choose one or you may compare two of them. This is to be written in your own words. Remember the issue of plagiarism!

Complete an annotated bibliography of five sources. An annotated bibliography is a list of sources providing complete bibliographic information along with a short description and evaluation of each source as it pertains to your topic. There should be at least <u>two</u> periodical articles, one book, and one web site. This bibliography will be due **Thursday, October 3,** and should be typewritten.

Your two names should go at the top, with "Annotated Bibliography" as the title. You will begin with the 2-3 information paragraphs on your topic. The five sources should be cited in correct bibliographic form, following MLA style. See the *library home page style guides* for examples of correct form or use a reference book that documents MLA style. Besides correctly formatting the individual sources the five works should be placed in alphabetical order by the author's last name. Below each title you should provide a three-to-four sentence annotation of each source.

Lynchburg College

COMM 101   Name _____

Before your class comes to the library for an orientation session, follow the instructions below and write your answers in the spaces provided.

Log-on to Expanded Academic ASAP, a cross-discipline index to current journals and magazines. If not familiar with the logon procedure, follow these instructions:

- At any LC campus networked computer, type the URL (address) for the Library's Desktop www.lynchburg.edu/library/eresource/eresource.htm OR you can log on to the Library's Homepage, www.lynchburg edu/library click on Library and Information Resources, then click on the Desktop URL in the center of the screen.
- Click on General Articles and then on Expanded Academic ASAP.

1. Select a topic you need to find articles on, preferably for this class, and click in the entry box and then type the main concepts of your topic. Write the terms you are searching here. _____
_____

Then click on Search.

How many articles were retrieved? _____If no matching citations were found, go back to the search screen and try searching again with fewer terms or try a new topic.

When you have a list of citations, look at the first 20 articles (this is the maximum that you can scroll through at one time). Don't worry if you have less than 20 citations, answer the questions as best you can. Print these citations (just the first 20 if you found more than that).

2. How many of the 20 citations appear (based on the article title and journal name) to be useful for your paper/speech? _____

3. How many are available in full text online? ("view text with graphics and retrieval choices" follows these citations)_____ How many are in journals that Lynchburg College subscribes to? (The citation is followed by a blue book with a yellow arrow) _____

4. Now click on the blue underlined phrase that follows one of the citations that looks interesting, go to the end of the article or the abstract if it is "abstract only" and find the list of subject headings that were assigned to this article. Write the one that you think will be the best one to look for more articles on your topic here _____
_____

5. In the blue column on the left click on **"return to: 'Search'** and switch to searching by subject headings by clicking on the "Subject Guide" bar in the blue column on the left. Type the subject heading selected in 4 in the search box and run the search. How many general articles does it retrieve? _____   If there is an option to **"narrow by subdivision"** click on the **narrow** and write the first subdivision here followed by how many articles are available under it.
_____

6. Open the list of general articles and compare the first 20 with the first 20 you found doing the keyword search. Which group has more articles that are actually on the topic you are researching?
Subject Guide _____ or Keyword search _____

7. How many of the subject guide search articles on the first page of citations are available in fulltext online? _____

8. How many are in journals subscribed to by Lynchburg College? _____

9. What is the primary concept of the topic you are searching? _____

10. What are the secondary concepts? (no more than 2)

_____

(For instance if I am doing research for a paper on "The influence of the deforestation of tropical rainforests on air pollution," my primary concept would be rainforests and my secondary concepts would be deforestation and air pollution.)

11. What other terms could you use to search for these concepts besides the ones you have already used? (Think synonyms or closely related terms, for instance for "deforestation" I could also use the term "logging.")

    Concept 1

_____

    Concept 2

_____

    Concept 3

_____

    If you have problems with any of these questions, we will be going over them when you come for your library session.

<u>BRING THIS SHEET WITH YOU TO THE LIBRARY!</u>

Marywood University

Steps for Selection
How to identify, locate, evaluate a periodical title

See <u>Research Guides</u> by subject   OR

Enter these terms for a <u>Subject Browse</u> search in **MELVIN**, the online catalog

_____ And "periodicals"
      (Subject)

At list of titles, highlight any two and "see details".

Scroll down to "subscription summary" and note the following-

For _____subscription is ____active ____inactive.
     (Title A)
Years covered – from _____to _____ Any title changes __yes _____ no

Title is available on microfilm _____yes _____no. Microfilm coverage - from _____ to_____

For _____subscription is ____active ____inactive.
     (Title B)
Years covered – from _____to _____ Any title changes __yes _____ no

Title is available on microfilm _____yes _____no. Microfilm coverage - from _____ to_____

Find an issue of <u>one</u> of the periodicals you selected above. (Bound or Current)

Based on the following criteria, is the journal scholarly or isn't it? (For more information on how to determine if a periodical is scholarly, general interest , trade, or popular see that section under Research Guides.)

_____Is the journal published or sponsored by a professional society?

_____Is there a list of reviewers (editorial board) inside the front cover or on first few pages?

_____Are its articles based on original research or by authorities in the field?

_____Do the articles begin with an abstract? _____End with a bibliography or list of references?

_____Are authors' credentials listed?

_____ Do article titles reflect content?

DATABASE EXPLORATION
User Evaluation Form

Name of Database:_____

Reason for Selection: _____
(Personal/Department research, General subject interest, Assessment for student/curricular use,
Other)

User's Level of Experience with the Database:_____
(No previous use, Some familiarity, Moderate experience, Advanced use)

Valuable Features: (Please check those which were most
apparent to you.)

_____Contents/Help?

_____Index

_____Thesaurus

_____Selection from multiple resources, possibility of simultaneous searching

_____Links to additional terms, key words, descriptors

_____Examples of searches

_____Full text

_____Key to local holdings

_____Search history

_____Other

Ease of Use: (Please check those which were most important to
you.)

_____Simple login

_____Clear and obvious arrangement of commands, examples, other components

_____Clear directions for entry of search terms, limiters, field terms

_____Ability to refine search easily

_____Options for display of partial/full screen citation, abstract, or full text

_____Obvious connections from each segment of the database to other segments

_____Clear choices for printing, downloading, e-mailing results

HONR111 BIBLIOGRAPHY EXERCISE 09/02

Citing your sources so that your reader can easily check them is one of the simplest and most important pieces of academic writing. Instructions for one of the most common citation systems, that adopted by the Modern Language Association, is found on pages 381-90 of your text, Rottenberg's <u>Structure of Argument.</u> This exercise requires you develop your research skills and to display the results with attention to detail.

Go to the library and find the sources listed below. Retrieve all the bibliographical information you will need, and then prepare a one page bibliography listing the sources according to the MLA format. In addition to the sources listed below, find two additional sources which relate to the topic revealed by what you find. One of the two additional sources should be a web-site. The other should be a magazine or newspaper article. These should be incorporated in the bibliography. Entries should be ordered alphabetically by author.

There are different sources for different students, but at least five other people will be chasing down the same ones you are. Don't leave this to the last minute. The assignment is due on Wednesday, the 25th of September.

One last proviso. This assignment is worth 5 % of your grade. Because the object of this exercise is to have you learn how to do research and prepare a flawless bibliography, there are two marks available to you - the full 5 % if you present me with a bibliography which is perfect, and 0 if your bibliography suffers from any errors or omissions. We will discuss the bibliography next week, and I encourage you to bring a draft to me by Friday September 20th. I will be happy to advise you about search techniques etc. You can, of course, consult with other people who are working on the same sources. However, you are responsible for any errors in your own bibliography, and you should not directly copy each other's work.

SOURCES

Klein's review article in <u>Business History Review</u> volume 75, number 2.

Helge Berger et al.in a 2001 issue of <u>The Journal of Economic History</u>
HG 4551.S4 1993

An essay on the causes and effects of exchange rate volatility in the book edited by Jacob S. Dreyer and some others published in 1982.

The section on the "United States of America" in <u>The Statesman's Yearbook 2001.</u>

The Research Process

Search Strategy Worksheet

Name: _____ Date: _____

Course/Instructor _____ Assignment Due Date: _____

Step 1: Summarize the Topic.

Clearly state your topic in one or two sentences: Be as specific as possible.

_____

_____

_____

Step 2: Identify the Key Concepts.

Underline the main ideas of the topic you have listed in Step One.

Step 3: Focus your topic.

List an aspect of your topic on which you want to focus (ex. Location, time period etc.)

_____

Step 4: Narrow or revise your topic if necessary, based on your focus from Step 3.

Please list the new topic sentence below.

_____

_____

Step 5: Select concept words/phrases

In the spaces below, list keywords and synonyms that represent your topic, keeping in mind that one idea can be expressed in different ways (example: college, university, school, higher education etc.).

_____

_____

_____

Step 6: Creating Search Statements

Please read the instructions on using *Boolean operators* and *truncation symbols* to create sample search statements.

Boolean Operators : The terms AND, OR, NOT are used within a search statement to narrow, broaden or eliminate a concept.

Examples:

OR: Classical OR Music finds books/articles that could be about classical architecture or could also be about rap music. The use of OR broadens a search.

AND: Classical AND Music finds books/articles that have both "classical" and "music" somewhere in the record retrieved and will therefore find many more books about the topic of classical music. The use of AND narrows a topic

NOT: Music NOT classical finds books/articles about music but leaves out all the books/articles with the word "classical" somewhere in the book/article records. Using NOT eliminates a concept from a search.

Combination Searches: *(Classical AND Music) NOT Bach* is a more complex search. It will locate articles/books about classical music, but will not include any about the composer Bach. The parenthesis keeps the two main concepts together during the search.

Truncation/Wildcard: Symbols such as * and ? are used in an online catalog or database in order to retrieve all words that contain a root of a word or segments of a word

Examples: sing* would retrieve sing, singing, singers, single etc.; wom* would retrieve women and woman.

Write possible search statements below by combining your keywords from Step 5. Make sure to use the Boolean operators (AND, OR, NOT) and truncation as needed to broaden or narrow your search.

_____

_____

_____

_____

_____

Created by Kerrie Danielle Fergen August 9, 2002 Note: This guide has been adapted from Washington State University Libraries and Humboldt State University Library.

University of North Carolina at Pembroke

ENG 105 Library Research Worksheet

1. Choose a topic that interests you (or that was assigned) and describe it in a couple of sentences:

2. Use a GENERAL ENCYCLOPEDIA (such as *World Book* or *Encyclopedia Britannica,* located in the Reference Collection, call number AE 5 ...) to find background information on your topic.

Read the entry on your topic carefully and make notes on what you have read. Write down the author, title, publisher, volume number and page number of the entry:

3. Look for your topic in a SUBJECT reference work (encyclopedia, dictionary, handbook, etc.).
    *Use the "Guide to the Library of Congress Classification of Books," on the back of Sampson-Livermore Library bookmark (located at the Reference Desk or in the Reference Information rack), for the call number area of the reference works on your topic.
    *Use the encyclopedia's index to locate the volume and page number.

Read the entry on your topic carefully and take notes on what you have read. Write down the author, title, publisher, volume number and page number of the information on your topic:

4. Use *The Library of Congress Subject Headings* (large, red books in the Ready Reference Collection) to find subject terms that best describe your topic.

    •You MAY want to begin with a broad topic such as DRUG ABUSE; choose the term in bold
        or
    •You MAY want to choose a narrower term (NT), a related term (RT), or a broader term (BT).
    •Do NOT use terms listed as "UF" (Used For)

    Write down one or two terms that describe your subject:

5. Search for your topic or term in **BraveCat** (the library's online catalog) to find citations to **books.** Access books through any university networked PC. Begin at the library's home page *(www.uncp.edu/library)* and click on **BraveCat.** The Library offers many Internet-accessed PCs in the Reference area as well as the computer lab.
> •Use the subject term(s) or a keyword you found in question #4.
> •To search, click on the type of search you want to do, (i.e., **Subject** or **Keyword),** then type the words in the text box. Press **Enter** or click **Submit Search.** Click on the desired title(s) to view the item record(s)

> **Write down the author, title, call number and location code of at least two books on your subject:**

Reminder: Below, be sure to check **BraveCat** to see if the Library subscribes to the publication in EACH of your citations, as well as where each is available (bound volumes, microfilm or current periodicals).

6. Access full text articles or citations to periodical articles through any of the library's Internet-accessed PCs. Begin at the library's home page *www.uncp.edu/library/* and click on **Electronic Resources.** Click on **Database Title** and then **EBSCOhost.** Select both **MasterFILE Premier** and **Academic Search FullTEXT Elite** and enter your topic or term.

> **How many records did you find on your topic? _____**

> • Follow the directions provided by the database software to view abstracts of articles or full text articles.
> • Mark the items for print, and follow the directions provided to execute the print option.

> **Print at least two citations to articles on your subject and attach the printout to this worksheet.**

7. Next, select a **subject** specific database, such as **PsycInfo** or **Social Work Abstracts,** and search for another **article** on your topic.
> **How many records did you find on your topic?**
> Follow the directions provided by the database software to view abstracts of articles or full text articles. Mark the items for print, and follow the directions provided to execute the print option.

> **Print at least one citation to an article on your subject and attach the printout to this worksheet.**

8. Using a print index such as *Readers' Guide to Periodical Literature, Humanities Index,* or *Criminal Justice Periodicals Index,* find a citation on your topic or a related subject and **write the citation below.** Print indexes are currently shelved at the end of the Reference Collection in *Print Indexes.*

9.Consult **BraveCat** to see if the Library subscribes to the periodical in each of your citations, as well as each journal location (current periodicals, bound volumes, or microfilm).

> **Read the articles carefully, taking notes on what you have read. Make a copy of the first page of each article and attach it to this work sheet.**

Research Writing 223
Finding Background Information
Research Assignment One (updated 9/11/02)

Name _____   Instructor _____

For best results, read this first!
The purpose of this worksheet is to lead you through the first part of the research process, finding background information. The strategies you learn in this and subsequent assignments will be applicable to almost any term paper or research project you encounter in your college courses. By following a search strategy that leads from background reading to books located with the online catalog to article citations indexed in periodical indexes, you can make the best use of the time you spend in the library. You will also learn to predict what kinds of information you can expect to find in different types of sources.

Please feel free to ask a librarian for assistance. If you cannot find sufficient information in any of the types of sources listed in this assignment, please consult a librarian. They will help you identify appropriate substitute sources.

Record below a reference to background information on your topic. To receive full points for your reference, it must be **correctly punctuated** (1 point), **include these essential elements** (1 point) and be in the following order (1 point): author(s) of article (first author's name is inverted), title of article, title of encyclopedia, editor, number of volumes in set, place of publication, publisher and dates. **Follow the example below, including punctuation.** Look at the end of the article for the author(s). If no author is given, begin the reference with the title of the article.

Sample encyclopedia reference

Appleby, Anthony J. "Fuel cell." McGraw-Hill Encyclopedia of Science and Technology. Ed. Elizabeth Geller. 20 vols. New York: McGraw-Hill, 2002.

ENCYCLOPEDIA REFERENCE IN BIBLIOGRAPHIC FORMAT (follow the above example)

3 _____

_____

List any additional terms you find in the encyclopedia that describe your topic.

1 _____

Does the encyclopedia article contain a bibliography which could lead to other resources? If so, note the author and title of a useful item in the bibliography.

2 _____

_____

Read this to find out which kinds of sources qualify as background sources.

Any relevant book or encyclopedia article is acceptable. Use the online catalog to find books and encyclopedias. If you cannot find any works on your topic, please ask one of the professional librarians for assistance. If no encyclopedia articles or books on your topic are in the library, the librarian will help you find a review article in a journal and initial your assignment. Review articles present overviews or summaries of what has been done in the field, not one opinion or one experiment on the topic.

This part on subject headings is critical for all your library searches. Read it!

In standard bibliographic format (different format from that used in the online catalog), record below one of the references listed in your search results from above. To receive full points for your references, they must be correctly punctuated, include the essential elements (1 point), and be in the following order (1 point): author or editor, complete title, place of publication, publisher, and date of publication. **Follow the example below, including punctuation.** For two authors, employ both (notice that only the first author's name is inverted); for three or more authors, use the abbreviation "et al." which means "and others."

Sample book references

Vincent and David Shiflett. Christianity on Trial: Arguments against Anti-religious Bigotry. San Francisco: Encounter Books, 2002.

Drexler, Madeline. Secret Agents: The Menace of Emerging Infections. Washington D.C: Joseph Henry Press, 2002.

SOURCE BIBLIOGRAPHIC FORMAT (may be an encyclopedia article or book)

3 _____

Does this article or book have a bibliography which could lead you to other resources? If so, note the title and the author of a useful item in the bibliography

2 _____

PART TWO: REFLECTION

_____ What seem to be the broad categories in your subject?

2

_____

_____ Summarize what you have learned about your topic thus far?
3

_____

_____

_____

_____ List any names that you found more than once in your research. These are likely
1 important people in the field. You should look for more of their articles and books later in your reasearch

_____

_____

_____

_____ What questions do you still have on your topic? (This will guide your searching in a subsequent
2 assignment.)

_____

_____

_____

_____ What questions do you have about doing research or using the library? Note: These are two free
2 points for you. If you don't have any questions, you haven't used the library enough! A response
indicating that you have no questions will not earn any credit.

_____

_____

_____